# MILLION

## HIGHLY SUCCESSFUL ENTREPRENEURS

# DOLLAR

## SHARE THE BEST ADVICE & SECRETS

# DADS

## FOR MASTERING WORK-LIFE BALANCE

WRITTEN BY

**PRESTON ANDERSON**          **CHRIS BADEN**

**ERIC BEER**     **JAMES GOLDEN**          **CODY LOUGHLIN**

**EVANS PUTMAN**          **AKBAR SHEIKH**

Editors: James Afolarin, Thomas Hauck
Book Design: Kristen Forbes (DeviancePress.com)
Cover Graphics: PixelStudio

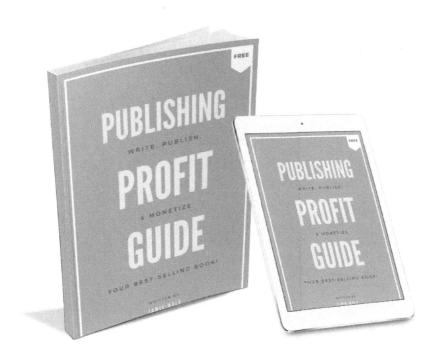

# DOWNLOAD YOUR FREE PUBLISHING PROFIT GUIDE!

This is my gift to you for buying this book

## TO DOWNLOAD, GO TO:
http://milliondollarstory.co/guide

# NOW IT'S TIME TO SHARE <u>YOUR</u> STORY

Become a bestselling author & significantly grow
your network of INFLUENCE!

We know how busy you are, so let us help you
write your story and get it published
as part of a bestselling book.

Do it **<u>TODAY</u>**

Go to:

http://milliondollarstory.co

People are waiting to hear your story…
it's time for you to share it!

# Contents

# Praise for **Million Dollar Dads**

*"These stories offer an amazing perspective that life is not easy, that life will throw you some huge curveballs, and you have to learn to overcome them. Running a business is the same as running your life. Husband, father, leader; each day is a new day with ups and downs. Your family, kids, or employees rely on you to make the best decisions. They need someone to look up to, to help them overcome, adapt, pivot, and solve those problems. This book provides the perspective that we are all humans, we all have feelings, we all bleed the same, and some of us have way more to juggle than others but we don't make excuses. We put our heads down and rise above the challenges. This book helped me realize I'm not alone in facing challenges and it's possible to balance family with work and still become successful. Have a blessed one!"*

- **Alex Cantaboni,** father, husband, and owner of Safe Pro Pest Control, www.SafeProPest.com

"What an incredible book! This collection of lessons on being both a dad and a business owner is one of the best I've ever read on the topic, and trust me, I've read a few! Wearing the hats of a dad and a business owner, I know all too well how tough it can be to separate the time, emotion, and stress of being a parent and a business owner. You do all you can to leave the frustrations from home at home when at the office, and the frustrations of the office at the office, when at home. Like this wonderful collection of dads, I do try to take away lessons from the business world and share them as educational moments with my kids. Sometimes those lessons make sense to them and sometimes they make no sense at all. In two of my companies, I work exclusively with other business owners. With a client base in the thousands, I can tell you that many other dads out there need to read this book! My clients routinely share the challenges of trying to be outstanding dads while doing everything they can to be the best business owners they can be. I'm so grateful that these gentlemen took their valuable time to write this book! I plan to purchase quite a few to give to my fellow dads from church, family, and also my clients."

- **Chris Clear,** Atlantic Merchant Services, LLC, Accurate Payment Solutions, https://atlanticmerchant.com/chrisclear/

*"Life is all about perspective. Our perspective comes from successes and challenges that we have faced or that other people have gone through that we are fortunate enough to learn from. Million Dollar Dads provides unique perspectivse from seven different entrepreneurs with their real-life stories of overcoming struggle and reaching the pinnacle of success in their respective industries. Their stories let us know that we are not alone in our search to find balance in our personal and professional lives."*

**- Chris Shortino,** Realtor at www.shortinogroup.com

*"I love a great success story. It's inspiring to learn about someone who is down on their luck being able to rise to make themselves a better business owner, father, and person altogether. I love reading about the struggle - about how bad it was and yet there was no blame and no jealousy of others. And then to feel their belief that they can, and will be, better in the future as they climb slowly to where they are today. My challenges may not have been as tough as some of the ones recounted in this book but I always knew it was up to me to make the changes needed to succeed. Over the last couple of years, I've studied self-help - reading books, listening to audiobooks, and applying the information in my daily practices. Then I started working with a*

3

*sales coach. It feels like everyone has that Ah-Ha moment. But it's what you do at that moment that makes all the difference in the world. Dream Big!!"*

- **Eric Rhew,** Branding Consultant Promo Logic
www.promologicllc.com

*"This book is outstanding at so many levels. Every upcoming entrepreneur needs to read this as it has real-life examples and situations that every single person can relate to on some level. Most entrepreneurs deal with similar obstacles in different situations where you get the urge to give up and settle. It's difficult to see the "other side" when you haven't gotten there yet. Having real-life everyday people just doing the best they can and overcoming obstacles gives you the exact motivation that you need. These husbands, fathers, and business owners have pursued the sometimes difficult balance of work-family lifestyle and now share their experiences to encourage others to succeed."*

- **Hayley Fisher-Martenson,** Mom, Wife, Owner at Fisher Business Solutions www.fisherbusinesssolutions. co and Manager/Broker at Blue Sky Benefit Solutions www.blueskybenefits.com

*"In Million Dollar Dads you learn real-life accounts of how everyday young entrepreneurs became very successful business-owning dads. One of the most stressful things in life is figuring out the balance between home and work. These Millon Dollar Dads do an excellent job of putting into perspective their struggles and successes on how to achieve the secret to this balance. This book hit home for me, and I highly recommend it to young entrepreneurial fathers."*

**- Jonathan Dwyer**

*"The stories in this book resonate with me and I felt drawn into them from start to finish. It is great to read about successful entrepreneurs, especially those willing to share their formula for success. It reminds me of myself when I lost my job a week before Christmas in 2017! If you love to read real-life stories of going from broke and defeated to a life of happiness and success then this is a great addition to your library."*

**- Patrick Bolanos,** Success Junky, Serial Entrepreneur, Co-Founder of Trailer King Builders, https://trailerkingbuilders.com/

*"As a father, it's hard to relate to all the big-time entrepreneurs who seem to have it all together. It feels to me as if they must not ever see their family. After reading Million Dollar Dads, I realize I can have it all. I can have a business and I can have a family; it just takes intention. I feel inspired to be a better dad and a better business owner. Anyone trying to balance being a dad and being a boss needs to read this."*

**- Trent Bray**

# Preface

Welcome to a gathering of Million Dollar Dads - highly successful Dad entrepreneurs who, in the following pages, will share their best advice and secrets for mastering work-life balance. This group of super-influencers and authors created this volume during ongoing months of uncertainty in the US and around the world. There have been so many "never before in history" events that it is almost overwhelming. Yet, this group of heart-centered, success-and-mission driven entrepreneurs is exceptionally motivated and well-positioned to have a huge impact in a hurry and they want you to succeed quickly, too.

These entrepreneur fathers are driven, goal-oriented providers. Success has been a constant motivator and many - not all - came from the competitive environment of sports. And yet, one topic that surfaces frequently is failure, while another is priorities. I believe you will find they all agree that failure is a wonderful teacher and never something to shy away from or judge yourself harshly for going through. Meanwhile, they all concluded that being present for family and making an impact starting at home is the reason they work so hard while now recognizing where to draw the line for attention and energy.

Parents want first and foremost to give our children hope, to paint for them a picture of a beautiful world and their place in it. Entrepreneurs focus on solutions so we view the upheaval as an opportunity for change and good, and we want our children to feel that, too - not in an opportunistic way but in a genuine way.

Now, more than ever, people need a way to support themselves and their families that doesn't depend on physically going to a job in which you work for someone else. Truthfully, the dad entrepreneurs in these pages felt early that they were wired differently, that they were hungry in such a way that being an employee couldn't satisfy. Because they carved a path and gained experience, they have well-earned advice to share with you if you are transitioning into entrepreneurship now. As one author stated, "Winners win," and they are here to help you achieve the work-life balance you seek. They also engage with their children to ensure that they are financially literate, solution-oriented, action takers... at any age!

We see this as a time for expansion, knowing that the more we grow our businesses the more people we can employ, which has a ripple effect throughout the economy; as husbands, fathers, businessmen, and leaders, there is a weight of responsibility to care for others in a huge way. And we certainly believe and accept the privilege of making more to give more.

Plus, when we give our children the tools to be intellectually and financially independent, we free them to stand tall and proud and able to confidently overcome barriers. When we follow through on huge dreams, we lead by example so that our children believe they can follow us courageously and enthusiastically. They know we make more money so we donate more to the people and organizations with the most urgent needs. So yes, there is opportunity and hope - even in, especially in - the midst of crisis.

We want to help! It is always what drives us. Better yet, we are perfectly positioned TO help! We've already struggled with doubt and overwhelm and come out the other side. We've already been subject to mindset challenges and to being unsure of what to do to help ourselves and others and we've come through to the other side. We've already navigated the logistics of learning what to do first, then next, and the logistics of implementing to get results over theory. You'll find as you read this book, we have chosen to be incredibly vulnerable with you so that you know whoever you are, wherever you are, and whatever life has thrown at you, we are certain you will get through to where you've always dreamed of being. We have enough belief to share; you can borrow ours until you've grown your own. We are here for you!

We aren't minimizing fear. We recognize there is real heartache, real loss, and real suffering. These dads are faced with the same current balancing act of having both parents working from home, all the kids home all day, needing help with online schooling, needing computers, taking up bandwidth, changing up schedules. It's all about perspective. The entrepreneurial journey teaches us the long game - just like being a son, brother, husband, father, business owner, investor, and philanthropist - permitting us to navigate highs and lows, believing with 100% certainty we don't need to wait for good times to return - we make good times now!

We've already seen connections multiply and been reminded to reach out more often to our friends, our neighbors, our family, and those who work tirelessly to heal us or keep us safe.

We have witnessed shifting priorities and in some ways have come to feel more grounded even during such upheaval. And we have become rabid consumers of content while searching for new ways to learn and to earn a living.

The following stories are powerful, transformative, and inspirational. My wish for you is that they nourish your belief, providing you with the courage to keep going in pursuit of your dreams - even if your dreams are forced in a new direction. And if you are still in school, virtually or otherwise, I hope you realize the only limits you face are ones you let yourself believe.

I invite you to discover how collectively we, as these authors demonstrate, may use our unique stories to change the world in small or large measure. Sometimes change is forced upon us. That has certainly been true lately. It can feel hard when we don't choose it; we can use energy to resist or energy to embrace change. Our authors - these dads and trailblazers who forge ahead - are here to help you use this pivotal period in history to build highly successful businesses and master work-life balance.

Each author has provided links to their information. Be sure to connect with them and let them help you today!

# Preston Anderson

## DO YOU WANT TO SAVE MONEY ON TAXES OR INCREASE YOUR NET WORTH?

*Preston "The Tax Genie" Anderson, CPA*
*President & Chief Tax Strategist of Anderson Tax*
*www.anderson.tax*

---

*"If you want to change your life, figure out how your worst day was your best day."*
Tony Robbins

*"You will get all you want in life if you help enough other people get what they want."*
Zig Ziglar

*"Wealth is never about what you do once but about what you do consistently."*
Preston Anderson

---

My story started when I was in kindergarten. I had a functional mathematical brain at a young age. I could do square roots and I knew how numbers worked. In second grade I started doing calculus so I've always known I was going to do something involving numbers.

Then, in high school, I discovered accounting, and because I loved numbers I started participating in accounting competitions. At the same time, I found out I had a stepdad who was doing taxes as a certified public accountant (CPA). And realizing what he did, at that moment I suddenly decided I was going to be an accountant, too. To me, taxes were the law of numbers.

So I went to college and got my Bachelor's degree in Accounting. After that, I proceeded to get my Master's degree in Taxes. Not an MBA, mind you; I studied taxes, not business. I did that because I loved numbers and the idea of helping people save money.

For the first ten years of my career, I believed that what I was doing was the pinnacle of what every CPA or tax preparer could do. I had the mindset that I was supposed to work for a thousand hours over ten weeks of tax season. I believed that I was going to prepare over a thousand returns in ten weeks and that I was always going to be talking about how hard I work.

Little did I know that what I was doing was just the basic grunt work of annual tax prep. Anyone could essentially get the full range of services similar to my efforts at an H&R Block. I know it's kind of insane if you think about it that way. I had undergraduate plus graduate training and yet, people who took a single 6-8 week course could perform essentially the same function I did. It was a jolt to discover our offerings were the same.

However, about seven years into my career I met four guys who changed my life. They called themselves 'tax planners' and I saw them help a client of mine save some money. It was not too much money — about $15,000 a year or so. Before this experience, I had that thought that saving taxes for my clients was about my outworking everyone. But, all of a sudden, I saw how these guys approached taxes differently while easily saving their clients money year over year. My first reaction to them was to ask if they were taking personal expenses and finding ways to deduct them. It was not; they were doing something entirely different related to creating deductions.

I asked them to explain further and to my surprise, they shared the strategy with me. When I understood their approach

I was interested and wanted to work with them. They told me as an accountant I couldn't do what they did. They were attorneys who offered tax strategy and planning.

So, because of my lemonade beliefs and mindset, I went back to preparing my thousands of tax returns and working 18 to 20 hours per day. I was killing myself with work and I hated my life. I hated it until the day I got into an argument with my boss. That was the day I told him I was done because I realized I truly was. I finally understood I was done working in a culture that equated working "more" with being "better."

Like many before me, I quit after reaching my breaking point and I quit without a plan. I had just purchased a house and I had a two-month-old son at home,  and I quit my job. That was how desperate and overwhelmed I felt.

Fortunately, because of my relationship with some of my former clients, I was able to start my firm relatively quickly. But even then, I still wasn't doing exactly what I wanted to do. From my first decision to become an accountant and focus on taxes, my goal had always been to help people save money. While I had instituted some tax plans and accomplished my goal for a few people, I started to understand my processes weren't very organized or systematized. Mostly I offered strategies and suggestions without taking a good look at the entire lives of my clients. I wasn't helping them as much as I could.

## THE CALM BEFORE THE STORM

I can remember a client I helped who was a doctor. He had three kids in "Ivy League" schools and was paying $50,000 in tuition per year per child. I was able to find a way to help him deduct taxes off that $150,000 and save him roughly $65,000 annually. Looking back, knowing all the things I know today, I believe I could have saved him a lot more. At that time, I still wasn't taking a holistic approach by looking at a client's entire set of activities.

Ironically, I started my business by building on the things I had learned from my previous boss, the one who brought me to the breaking point. I already knew how to market myself by talking to business owners, attending Chamber of Commerce meetings, and doing other business networking. My business grew consistently just from doing what I knew and my firm was doing multiple six figures.

The challenge of getting comfortable when things are going well enough is that you aren't motivated to look for what could be done better. Things were good for a while but it didn't take long before I started having problems. When my son - who had been just two months old when I started my firm - turned three, he went blind and we discovered that he had six congenital heart defects. The center of our lives moved to the hospital.

One of the networking organizations I belonged to, one that was the primary source of my business growth to that point, had a very strict attendance rule. Because of my son's illness, I no longer met their requirements and they terminated my membership. I had no idea what to do next.

About three weeks later I found an ad for a digital marketer. I watched it and thought, "Holy smokes!" This is exactly what I need! I was eager to dive into it with the marketer and told him I wanted to work together as soon as possible.

But after the tax season my son had his second open-heart surgery and it didn't go well. He ended up having a three-month consecutive stay at the hospital. One day my wife called me saying, "You need to get to the hospital now!" When I arrived I saw about 20 nurses and doctors working furiously in his room. A nurse escorted me out of the way and I can remember just sitting there not knowing what to do.

Over the next few weeks, my son's situation was exactly like that. We had good days and bad days, although to be honest, the majority were bad ones. During that time my son was on an iron lung. Over the next year, he was in the hospital more often than he was home. He'd be hospitalized for five weeks, come home for three days, get sick, and then we'd have to rush him back to the hospital.

That was the situation I found myself in. I had a son in the hospital and I was trying to grow my business. Unfortunately, I didn't know how to deal with stress very well. I started detaching myself from my family in an unhealthy way, spending hours playing video games. Meanwhile, I found solace at work because it was the one place in my life where I had some control. I hired my first business coach who helped me triple my business in two years.

But it was a very hard time for my wife because I was not present and I wasn't helping out in the many ways I should have. Then the situation got worse when my son had another episode. His heart stopped the day before the date he was scheduled for a tracheotomy procedure. It was a week before taxes ended and yet again, I felt lost. I did the only thing I knew how to do; I decided to work. As my son had his third open-heart surgery and my wife sat at the hospital, I was at the office working.

And that was when I realized my priorities were way off.

Yes, I can make more money and do people's tax returns and planning, but I wasn't taking care of my family. I had made business decisions at the expense of my family. When my son eventually came home, the third surgery proved to be successful. It fixed him completely and he started to get better. But just as he started getting better, I started falling apart.

This is because when we first learned of his illness, I stopped taking care of myself. Now that he was getting better, all the pain and emotion I hadn't allowed myself to feel started surfacing and I went through a massive depression. The result was that I decided to sell my business.

There's an old saying, "No success in business will ever make up for failures at home." So, in October 2018, I sold my business and moved on. A lot of clients were very upset with me and I had so much anxiety I couldn't talk to people. I knew I was making more money than most people ever dreamed of, but I had to let it go so I could reconnect with my family. I had to dump everything and start over.

# MAKE MORE MONEY TO KEEP MORE MONEY

My number one mission now is to reduce the taxes of every single client I work with. I am a CPA but I like to call myself a "tax genie."

People often tell me they have made some money and want to know how they can make their taxes go to zero. My reply to them is that this is the wrong question. The question shouldn't be how to get your taxes to zero, it should be how to keep most of your money. There's a subtle difference in there but it matters.

There is a lot of poor financial advice circulating. If you look at taxes from the angle of getting your taxes to zero, the obvious solution is to spend more. Unfortunately for most people, that's exactly what most accountants recommend. They'll tell you to spend more: give more money to charity, buy equipment, and expense as much as possible. If your tax bracket is 30% and you buy a piece of equipment for $10,000, you will be able to "save" $3,000 - but of course, you are still out a net $7000. If that new equipment makes money for your business, that's great. But you won't always need new equipment. Timing is therefore very important with my clients' plans.

## JUMPING OVER DOLLARS TO SAVE PENNIES

For instance, a client came to me because all his income deductions had been attributed to a single tax year. I reviewed his filed tax returns and determined that his accountant had been too aggressive in lowering his taxes. I was able to move $150,000 out of that year into the following year. By doing that, his income went up to $150,000 and it cost him about $5,000 in taxes for that year. However, in the following year when his income was considerably higher, he saved $70,000 net. The goal of tax reduction is to save money over years, not reduce any one year to zero tax liability.

I always tell people that the goal of tax planning is to create a higher net worth both in the current year and for your entire lifetime. You don't want to take a position that will benefit you in the present and hurt you over the long run. Your goal should be to keep more of your money.

I had a client who sold his business for $15 Million and ended up owing the IRS $2 Million. He made the mistake of stepping over dollars to collect pennies. He had a plan that saved him about ten grand a year for about ten years. But saving $100,000 ultimately cost him $2,000,000. With proper planning, he could have received the entire proceeds from selling his business essentially tax-free, paying zero in taxes at the time of sale.

This is my goal with every client. I don't just try to lower taxes; my goal is to ultimately increase net worth. Saving on taxes in any one year doesn't increase net worth; investing does. Follow Jeff Bezos and Warren Buffet's model of investing; it is all about investing with discipline and consistency.

The problem with many people is they want to get rich overnight. Everyone is looking for shortcuts these days. However, the key to creating long-term wealth is consistency, both in earning and investing. Wealth is never about what you do once but about what you do consistently.

It will be very hard for you to set aside 10% of your income for investment out of the blue. But, it's not so hard to set aside that 10% if it is done monthly. It becomes even easier if that 10% is deducted automatically. Employing automation means you don't have to think about your taxes or investments, allowing you to stay consistent which is key.

Let's say you have a goal to save $50,000. You can break it into twelve payments of about $4,000 each month. But, it's best to do it in a way you don't see it. Make it so you don't have to think about it before the money is deducted from your account and then you won't miss it. As I said earlier, consistency is the key to success and higher net worth. But, if consistency is the key, automation is the tires that make it go around.

Accounting and investing can be hard to navigate for the average person and therefore it can feel as if there are barriers between you and your goals. Automation takes all the barriers away.

My hope is for my clients to stay consistent, update their books, and invest every single month to stay on track. But, life is busy and that's why I automate everything. Don't think about credit card payments, personal finance, mortgages, or revolving debt. Set it up in such a way that everything is paid automatically. The Quickbooks I use are 100% automated and I just have to log in and reconcile the books. It only takes me about five minutes a month and you can set your finances up this way, too.

Your takeaways here are automation and consistency. Now let's talk about discipline because when you bring self-discipline to money the payoff is worth it. When you set boundaries around yourself, it creates freedom around everything in your life. A lot of people see discipline as a burden, but it's not.

For example, many people look at their finances and think on a very short and limited timeline such as how much they got paid last week. More informed and disciplined people think of the future. I encourage my clients to consider a three-generation timeline; this is legacy-making! I ask them to consider how their work can benefit future generations.

## KNOWING THE IMPORTANCE OF OFFERING VALUE

That year after I sold my business, I went to work on improving my relationship with my wife. I did this because I decided to make it my absolute priority. While my situation began to improve, some of my professional relationships were damaged.

Before I sold my first business, I was getting a new referral every single week. That pipeline suddenly stopped, forcing me to find a new way of marketing for my next business. Because of that, success did not come as quickly as it had the first time. I had to go through a long period of learning. I hired coaches but found their suggestions didn't align with my ethics. I realized that real, genuine business is about giving value. And as soon as I learned that and started giving value to my clients, everything changed for me.

I remember seeing a Facebook post in which someone asked a tax question. It was frustrating to see so many respond with comments devoted to selling themselves rather than giving accurate and helpful information. I simply answered the question in such a way that I gave value rather than trying to sell myself. I thought it would be a one-time thing, but all of a sudden I was getting more than a hundred facebook requests a day. I realized I had unlocked something that day, and since then I've changed my entire marketing model.

Rather than telling people what I do, I provide solutions to their problems instead. People don't care about my skills; they care about making their problems get resolved. I give as much value as I can to my clients. Sometimes, I even anticipate their problems and suggest solutions before they discover the problems.

I let people see that what I bring to a business is different from other accountants and tax planners. I am value-driven in my work and my mentoring and I teach others to be the same. Perhaps if you can provide a solution in one aspect you can be the one to help with other problems, too.

As a CPA I can provide concise, clear directions, and even give you my entire process and strategies. But information alone can be overwhelming without someone to walk you through each step. In the past, I used to be afraid to give everything and I would want to take something. In other words, I would promise to solve solutions but only if I first sold someone something. Everything changed after my son's experience. Now I connect to provide value. People recognize and appreciate that I am being genuine and it causes people to reach out to me because they've seen they can trust me. It's a much different conversation when clients come to you and it places you in a stronger position to grow your business and influence.

## OPENING YOUR MIND TO THE POSSIBILITIES

Over the years I've experienced many successes and yet my focus was still fairly narrow, equating working many hours and processing lots of returns to short-term gain for both myself and my clients. When my son got sick, I began to lose myself. I happened to read "The Secret" and even though I don't follow the Law of Attraction, the book did cause me to think differently than I had previously.

I began to see the possibilities I hadn't previously noticed. Before reading that book, I was floundering. Since then I've become a student of growth and gratitude mindsets and I've been able to flourish - to become my best self. I am now devoted to being the best entrepreneur, the best advisor I can be to my clients, and the best father and husband I can be to my loved ones. I believe you can, too.

The first shift to practice is called "Reframing." For some reason back then, every time my counselor talked about self-care, I would break down and begin to cry. I didn't know why I did this and my counselor couldn't figure it out either. It was only after I brought it up with one of my coaches that he advised me to flip it and make it into a strength.

He told me to change the way I framed my thoughts about a particular situation, and that was what I did. Reframing is just like putting on a new set of glasses. Instead of going with the idea that you will hate something, you go with the idea that you are going to love it because it's good for you. With the help of reframing, self-care suddenly became a strength instead of a struggle for me.

For instance, I used to struggle with running. I would run for a week or two and then I wouldn't run for a month because it felt hard. Then I chose to reframe how I thought about it.

I told myself I was going to enjoy the process of running. One year later, I completed the Chicago marathon and I have been running ever since! Reframing has been the key to so much in my life and it can be the same for you. Whenever I'm struggling with anything, I just say, "Okay, I'm going to reframe this."

This has been transformative for my clients and me. I listen to motivational speakers like Zig Ziglar and Earl Nightingale daily. Listening, taking notes, and consciously practicing reframing has helped me on my journey.

I've also learned to allow myself to be vulnerable. I'm now very open about my highs and lows. I'm willing to show people where I've been, where I'm going, and share my entire journey. Five years ago, I couldn't get out of bed. Today I'm running marathons and I'm becoming a true business leader.

My actions, my transparency, and my attitude of delivering value draw people to me. People reach out to me who need a lifeline and want me to teach them. I'm a CPA doing a lot of tax plans and tax work but in addition to my accounting work, a lot of my clients get mindset coaching that helps them grow as people.

# CHANGING YOUR MINDSET ABOUT SUCCESS AND FAILURE

Your mindset is crucial to your success in life; your reaction to success matters. For example, I have had clients who experience generating an income of $30,000, $50,000, or $100,000 per month. If they view that amount as life-changing, they'll start struggling to replicate it. Some get lazy after their big payday. They relax and downshift. The result is predictable. However, if you accomplish things that are out of your comfort zone, and choose to view them as normal you will continue to do the work, continue to push yourself to grow, and continue to succeed.

Your reaction to failure matters, too. Before, when something did not go my way, I placed all the blame on myself and labeled myself a failure. It was a fragile mental state and I had to struggle through it. The fact is that by trying new things and choosing to grow, you are always going to fail. It's like riding a bike. If you are not willing to scrape a knee, you won't learn and grow your skills.

Failure is a learning opportunity and it's not permanent. If something doesn't work, you can always find something that will. The key is to choose not to stay with the familiar; you'll be able to learn and grow and become a better person because of failure.

Finally, let's talk about gratitude. As Tony Robbins says, "How can the worst day of your life become the greatest?" My answer is simple: gratitude. I am thankful for everything I've got in my life, including the hardest times and my lowest moments. Without "the worst day" moments of my life I couldn't have reached the peaks. Back when things were good enough personally and professionally, I didn't know to be grateful and I didn't know I could do and be better.

When my son was born and then diagnosed, all that was disrupted. I was forced out of complacency; I had to start from scratch and take a hard look at my life. So, I'm grateful for the hardest times of my life because they've made me who I am today. They placed me on the path that led to where I am today. To improve your life, be willing to reframe your perception, view success as normal, see failure as an opportunity to learn, and be grateful for the lows as they will lead to the highs, which will seem so much more precious!

## MIXING BUSINESS AND FAMILY

As an entrepreneurial dad, I have learned a lot of key lessons over the years. Three years ago, my life was upside down and only my business worked. But, over the past year and a half, I've learned to take care of my mind and my family. I began meditating and I've come to realize that once the internal issues are fixed and you can breathe, the external issues get fixed as well.

Because I took care of my internal issues, my business flourished. I've also been able to help others with their problems in their business, personal life, and family life.

I've felt as if I've learned what this life is about…. Life is all about growing through adversity. It's not just about going through struggles. It's about trying to reach that absolute human peak of progress. In the last two years, I've tried to live this philosophy and I've been able to help others live it as well. So many times people think wrong when they want to manifest something in their lives. They try to manifest $100,000 and once they get it, they realize that the money didn't make them happy. They realized it's the experience and memories of going through a tough time that matter.

This is what I want you to take away. Life is truly about the struggle, the journey, and our connection and not the destination.

Preston

# Chris Baden

## WHAT IF YOU APPROACHED PROSPECTING WITH CHILDLIKE FAITH?

*Chris Baden, CEO, and Co-Founder of Sales Ascenders*
*www.SalesAscenders.com*

---

*"To accomplish something greater than yourself, it will take more than yourself."*

Chris Baden

---

Over the last five years, I have been involved in the building of three companies that did over $1 million in sales in three different industries (insurance, eCom, and software.) One of the core skills that has helped me build profitable businesses in any industry is prospecting. Prospecting is the first step in the sales process; it involves identifying potential customers - prospects - and converting them into paying clients. Prospecting has been powerful for me.

So it's a principle I would like to pass on to my kids. I call the kind of prospecting I do Purpose Driven Prospecting and it differs from conventional methods of acquiring customers. Some believe that great prospecting is all about being a smooth talker, a fantastic conversationalist, and a knowledgeable representative who can speak about product features and benefits. To be fair, I believe this method still works some of the time. But I don't think it's the best.

Also, there is another school of thought on prospecting. Some people say, "Don't get lost in features and benefits... Start with your why!" Their point is that you have to share your story of WHY the product/service is relevant to you. I believe this is another powerful way to go about prospecting. But, it's also not the best.

The problem with both of these prospecting methods is their focus; these two methods focus on the product and the sales professional. I like the focus to be on the prospect (the customer) when I'm prospecting. I've realized that it takes less effort, speeds up the sales cycle, and creates an improved personal experience for everyone involved.

The fact is that nobody cares about you, the product or

the service, and that's okay. What everybody cares about are their problems and how you can help them in finding solutions. Further, It's been my experience that not only knowing the problems but also understanding how your prospect feels about those problems. Identifying the major pain points and major emotions tied to that pain is key for effective prospecting!

After doing this, my work becomes easy. I can simply have a conversation and, through my questions, I will learn if a prospect is right for the sale. It's very soul-draining and expensive on the backend of the business to try selling to the wrong person. If you understand this, you will never want to work with the wrong customer again.

This is why Purpose Driven Prospecting is the only way out for me. This prospecting strategy keeps the focus on prospects and it asks people the following questions:

- What are your plans?

- What are your problems?

- What are you working through right now?

With Purpose Driven Prospecting, you can meet people where they are, and by doing so, they will talk more freely and open up way faster. You'll then be able to ask more questions to understand where they are, and you'll never get stuck in "Sales Jail." Sales Jail is the salesman's nightmare; it is having to do endless follow-up while ultimately being ghosted.

## SEEING PROSPECTING IN AN ENTIRELY NEW WAY

To see prospecting in a new way, you will need an entire shift in your perspective. This is why you need to meet Emmett, a three-year-old on a mission. He wants nothing more than to get a green Power Ranger but he is faced with a massive obstacle - he needs money to buy the toy.

Emmett happens to be my oldest son. One day, he came bursting into my office with excitement and a sense of newfound revelation. He told me, "Dad!!! I want a toy!" Finding that hilarious, I matched his energy and quickly responded, "That is GREAT!" He excitedly clarified that the toy he had his sights set on was a green Power Ranger. I affirmed his desire but with a catch, "Absolutely!" I said, "Once you get enough money, you can buy one right away!"

Some people look at me in a funny way when I share this story with them. They ask me, "Why are you making your three-year-old work?" They also ask me, "What can a three-year-old do to earn money?"

I see their concerns or objections as a problem. I wonder where these lame and disruptive thoughts come from. It's sad because I realize the culture around us seeds these doubts. However, I have committed to never being the voice that speaks in a limiting way in my kid's life. I'll never tell him he is too young or that he can't do anything. Thoughts like these make me nauseous and uncomfortable.

If my son wants to start a business then we are going to start a business. While the world might be busy thinking he is too young, I ignore that view because my son and I stay engaged in solving problems, serving others, and making money.

What I do instead is help my kids discover all the temporary limitations that we face in life and then we overcome them together. I also tell my kids they need to solve problems because I think there is a message in this for everyone.

Tell me, isn't it the truth that we experience temporary limitations at all stages of life? The major question is how we respond to those limitations because we all have two choices: We can stop and turn off our brains… OR… we can stay engaged and in the fight!

I want the second option for my kids. I want my son to

have the skills, wisdom, awareness, and necessary HABITS of staying engaged and in the fight. I don't want his brain to shut down when he encounters a limitation. I want his brain to automatically switch to solution mode and always find the YES that conquers the NO. I am committed to being the voice that supports my kids through all the obstacles they face, and to be there alongside them as they work through their challenges. I hope you are, too.

## POVERTY STARTS IN THE MIND

Back to our story, I realized that as soon as I mentioned money to him, his excitement began to dissipate. But, he then surprised me by asking me the question, "Dad, how do I get the money?" You might see no significance in this but I do. The cool thing about this question is that it's a "wealthy" question.

What are "wealthy" questions? Wealthy questions are valuable questions that lead to wealthy answers, thoughts, and outcomes. Wealthy questions are one of the core features of a wealthy mind.

In this world, not all minds are created the same; we have poor minds and we have wealthy minds. When those with poor minds and wealthy minds face the same financial obstacles, they respond predictably differently. You need to take note of this so you can make sure your mind is always wealthy. The first thing the poor mind typically does is reactively speak! The first thing a wealthy mind does is ask a valuable solution-oriented question. The focus here is on the "How can I?" And that's quality thinking at it's finest.

By asking how he can get money, Emmett is exercising his wealthy mind and his persistence by thinking through his financial obstacle. I then encourage him a bit further by telling him he can simply solve problems for other people and people will give him money for doing so.

As soon as he hears that he lights back up and starts walking to the door, but then he suddenly stops in his tracks and surprises me by asking, "Well Dad, how do I solve problems for other people?"

I was stumped at that point. Think about it. How do I help a three-year-old solve problems for other people and start a business? There is no easy answer to that and the answer didn't come to me immediately. Now, there's a lesson for you. A lot of people quit early when they are looking for ideas and solutions to their problems. Experience has taught me that patience and persistence are key. Sometimes, you can't just ask how you will do something once or twice but instead must ask yourself hundreds of times. The repetition forces your brain to work through the question over and over again. Every time you ask it the same question, it will be forced to generate more developed thoughts and answers.

Another takeaway for you is that the best businesses are usually the simple ones and they revolve around solving a problem you have faced. If you take a look at top businesses, you'll realize the problem is personal for the founder and that he or she simply responded to their own need by developing teams and systems around solving the same problem for other people.

Therefore, if you have ever felt lost in your business or if you have forgotten why you are running your business or why your customers should care, try to remember this point - the best business revolves around solving a personal problem.

That said, Emmett's business idea presented itself to us later that day. We were going out on a family errand but for some reason, we could not find our keys. When life brings us problems, they often come with bad feelings such as frustration, fear, and anxiety. However, I've learned that if we can get past these initial bad feelings, we will be able to connect with the gift hidden in the problem.

That was how I had the idea that became Emmett's first business. I said, "Hey Emmett, we need to make massive key chains so other people don't lose their keys like us. We can help solve this problem for others."

Again, he lit up like a Christmas tree and wasted no time. He started making keychains as soon as I suggested it. He acted immediately and, with the help of his mom, he was able to put together a leather key chain with a little loop on it. He even painted it.

*Emmett and his mom putting together his giant leather key chain*

Now think about this. What about you? What have you been doing? How many times have you had an answer right in front of you? How many times have you questioned your idea, picked it apart, overthought it, and had the breakthrough idea turn into an emotionally nagging idea that sucked your confidence and joy away?

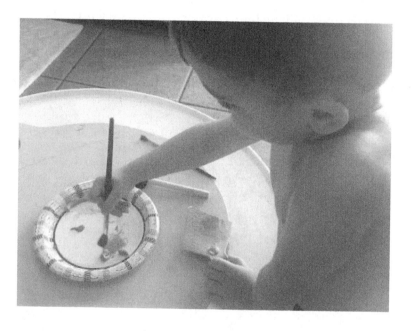

*A modern-day Picasso!*

The point I'm making here is that you have to take action. Even a small one will relieve some of your mental and emotional burdens. Emmett inspired me because he jumped right in. And I won't say he made an amazing piece of art. I won't say that his handcrafted leather has an exquisite gradient tone or that he is a modern-day Picasso. I'm not the kind of parent that thinks their kids' works are perfect just because they are my kid.

I mean no disrespect to my son, but his key chain looks exactly like a three-year-old dribbled paint on leather. The only thing that is noteworthy and admirable is that he followed his child-like faith. He took action and built his imperfect product with joy and love. And even though the product wasn't perfect, it fulfilled its intended purpose.

So I have a few questions for you. How much faster would you work if you did so with a little more childlike faith? How much faster would you work if you took more imperfect actions? If you kept a lighthearted process and treated your products/ services with more honesty, joy, and love, how would it affect your sales? Your team? Your fulfillment? Wouldn't it bring more energy and anticipation? Wouldn't we all be better off?

## LEARNING TO DEAL WITH DISCOMFORT

In this section, you'll learn one of the three major connections in life. You can download our entire process for bringing a new product to the market. It is this same process that we used for our newest mastermind and we did over $100,000 on its initial launch with zero money spent on ads. It turns out that when you do your market research and get all the answers, business isn't so hard. It's fun.

Now back to Emmett's story. The fact is that the world will always inform you of every possible limitation. I can't stop the world from telling my son that he is too young, too soft, thinking too big, or his ideas won't work, and so on. All I know is that I won't be that voice in his life. When he says he wants to climb to the top of the mountain, I say, "Let's figure it out."

This is who I am. When the world says eat sugar and con- venience foods, instead I figure out how to appreciate food, be grateful for it, and enjoy it without negative consequences. Words cannot describe what the word NO does to me; all kinds of resistance flows through me. I never want to hear that I can't do anything.

What we all need is the 'solution' voice. You need to have that voice that tells you that you can - and that encourages you to work towards what can be. Something that helps with this is changing your focus from goals to outcomes. I've realized that often goals are wishful thinking in disguise. With a goal-oriented mind, you can say, "Well the goal is this - let's see what happens." Thinking this way doesn't get things done and that's why focusing on outcomes is better.

Outcomes pose a different question to our brains. When you are outcome-oriented, you will start asking how what you want gets done. By focusing on outcomes, you will go the extra mile to ensure the desired result happens because an outcome is non-negotiable. It's about meeting a standard… and standards get met.

What's crazy about this story you are reading is that Emmett's motivation drove the whole thing. Sure, I provided some structure and his Momma provided support, but it went very fast all because of him. We never had to make him do anything. He just said 'yes' to the idea and got it done because he wanted his Power Ranger.

So at this point in the story, his product is built and the only thing left to do is get his market pitch down. By now, you are probably thinking, "Chris, you are nuts. Are you making your three-year-old solve a problem, build a product, memorize a pitch, and go door-to-door to make a few bucks just to buy a toy? Why on earth would you do this?" If you are asking that, the answer is simple. Isn't this the world we live in? We all work to eat, don't we? So why not learn the process sooner rather than later?

I helped Emmett get his pitch down to, "I'm Emmett and I help people not lose their keys." So now it was time for us to go door-to-door. I know the reason most people don't do this is that it's uncomfortable. Saying the truth, it was uncomfortable for us at first.

The reason prospecting is so uncomfortable is because it becomes one of our greatest teachers in the business world. In seconds, it exposes the weaknesses of your product. Sometimes, even the thought of prospecting is enough to scare people to rethink their products and services.

I think this nervousness is good. I don't think the feeling is supposed to go away, which is why I've learned to embrace it. I believe it's this nervous energy that keeps our brains alive and actively focused on solving the problem of what to say and how to say it.

Another major reason for this restlessness is the anticipation of rejection. Prospecting comes with all the hardship, emotional punches, and baggage people throw at you. And you have no option but to push through. When talking with someone you haven't met before, it is easier for them to be less filtered. So people often say things directly and more rudely than they normally would. It's similar to the case of "keyboard courage" on social media, where people leave comments they say in person to someone.

I have done plenty of cold calling throughout my career and I can say that it hasn't changed. I get a restless feeling in my gut each time. You know, that restlessness that feels like you're about to be sick. This time around, my feelings are a lot worse because I know that I have to watch my son go through it.

## START WITH THE COLDEST CALL

We got no answers to our knocks on the first two doors. I noticed he was starting to get confused at this point because of something I did; I made sure we didn't go to people we knew. We went to 'cold' doors because I wanted him to learn to build a business of solving a problem others wanted to be solved.

If I had taken my three-year-old to neighbors who knew us, they might have felt obligated to buy from him just because we knew each other. I want his business to be real - and there is another lesson in this for you.

A lot of people who launch new products choose to start with friends and warm markets. It is advisable to go to the coldest market you can find. Why? Because they are the most honest. And the reason honesty matters is because honesty gives you speed. Strangers will give you honest feedback rapidly and that data can be used to fine-tune your ideas and products.

So, throw that fear out of the window and go have those cold conversations. By doing so, you'll be able to learn faster, serve at a higher level, and become profitable faster. If you would like access to the exact prospecting process I use, leave a private message on Facebook for me with the message, "Prospecting process."

So, that's the reason we went to 'cold' doors. Luckily, on our third try, the door opened and Emmett delivered his pitch, "I'm Emmett and I help people not lose their keys." But we were in for a surprise because the person's response was to say, "No thanks." He also introduced himself as Jim.

I reckoned my son did a great job with his pitch. But this guy looked him in the eyes and said, "No." While I was tempted to tell him he was a horrible human being, I had known rejection was going to happen at some point so I was prepared. I did what dads do; before Emmett has a chance to respond, I said with enthusiasm, "Emmett! Did you hear what he said? He doesn't have a problem losing his keys. Now we can just go help the next person who does have that problem!"

He was smiling once more as he said, "Okay!" He waved and said goodbye to Jim, jumped back into the wagon, and off we went to the next door. Now I want you to notice some facts. Did you notice the difference between what Emmett did and what people normally do? You'll notice that Emmett did not rethink his product or over-analyze his pitch. He didn't get embarrassed, ashamed, or slip into self-doubt. He didn't question the process or think his keychain wasn't cool enough.

What he did was turn back, wave to Jim saying, "Bye Mr. Jim have a nice day!" and happily headed to the next door. I believe there is something powerful in responding with love to those who reject you. It's easy to love only those who love us, but ask yourself, are you loving those who reject you in practical ways?

You can say you have seen too much or that you have been hurt too deeply. What I like to say is that "Joy is a choice." Yes, people can say hurtful things and reject you. But what they can never do is take away your joy. Joy leaves the day you give it away, and the good news is that you can take back your joy the second you want it.

So, after dealing with the rejection the best way I could, we continued our journey. As we were walking down the driveway to the next house, a bug truck (a pest control truck) pulled up and parked by the curb across the street. The driver exited the truck, looking and moving directly towards us. I told Emmett that we might as well go see if he needed a key chain.

On reaching him, Emmett delivered his pitch once again and he lifted the key chain he made to show the pest control worker. The man smirked a little bit and asked how much the key chain cost. My son told him it was $3. On hearing that, he looked at my son and then at the keychain and then dug out $3 from his wallet and handed it to Emmett. He closed the deal!

*Emmett with his brother and his new $3!*

However, because a green Power Rangers toy cost more than $3, we had to go out prospecting multiple times. The crazy thing about our journey is that each time we went out to sell, we had our biggest breakthrough after experiencing rejection.

*Notice Emmett made $10 on this sale!*

## BEING AN ENTREPRENEURIAL FATHER

There are three jars at my home: the first is the 'checking' jar, the second the 'savings' jar, and the third is the 'giving' jar. We have three jars because I believe in the tradition of saving and giving.

After Emmett earned enough money for his toy, the last step before he could purchase it was to put money in the jars.

He gave 10% of his earnings to both the 'savings' and the 'giving" jars. What was remaining could be deposited into, and withdrawn from, the 'checking' jar - and it was enough to purchase his green Power Ranger. It was time to get the toy and he was so excited!

*His Green Power Ranger arrived!*

Since then, I have constantly been finding ways for Emmett to solve more problems because he wants more toys. He is currently working on a business that has a recurring service that makes him $30 per month. I would never have guessed where this would have led and I still don't know where it is going. But

I can say it's made a lasting impression.

There is no way to describe the impact this experience with my son has had on me. Relearning the principles and power of prospecting through the eyes of a three-year-old brought back so much clarity. It reminded me of how simple business and making connections are.

It also made me understand why others are so afraid of prospecting. When faced with prospecting, a lot of questions pop up because of those uncomfortable feelings. We start asking the 'what if' questions:

- What if I get rejected?

- What if I don't say the right thing?

- What if my product isn't good enough?

- What if I'm not good enough?

A powerful thing I've learned is to change these poor mindset 'what if' questions to 'wealthy' mindset ones. If you are going to play the crappy 'what if' game, then you must play it on the positive side. Most of these questions are made-up anyway, so don't only make up the bad ones and talk yourself out of doing the work you know will change your life for the better. Instead, ask better questions like the following:

- What if prospecting today sparks confidence I have never felt before?

- What if my encounters today bring more momentum?

- What if prospecting creates the clarity that I've been needing for months and years?

- What if I make the one connection today that will change the very course of my life for the better?

As you can see, it's all about your mindset and how wealthy you keep it. And finally, I hope you have three big takeaways from this chapter:

1. You never look at prospecting the same

2. You are sold on the idea that to accomplish something greater than yourself, it will take more than yourself… this is practically created through the power of, and value in, connecting with others

3. You leave this chapter with two practical tools/

methods you can apply and reapply immediately in your business and see quick results!

In closing, I'm grateful for the authors, speakers, artists, entrepreneurs, coaches, and leaders who have answered the calling to prospect in this manner. I believe this is prospecting from the perspective of accomplishing something greater than ourselves. It's prospecting with the perspective that we have something to give.

Life is short and it's a gift and I can't wait to see what the gift of today brings. For me, it is Purpose Driven Prospecting. And we strongly recommend you try it out because it's probably going to change your life. You can stay connected with me at Salesascenders.com and on Facebook where you can ask to join our group, "Sales Ascenders Inner Circle"

Chris

# Eric Beer

## HOW DO YOU MAKE AN IMPACT AND BUILD A LEGACY?

*Eric Beer, CEO of Universal Marketing Partners, Host of Performance Marketer Podcast*
*UnivMP.com*
*www.ericbeer.com*

*"Everything Is Measurable. Results Matter!"*

Eric Beer

I'm a married man - my wife's name is Ali - with two lovely kids: my 12-year-old son, Zach, and my 15-year-old daughter, Ashley. My story starts back in high school. I played sports as a kid, and back then I thought I would grow up to be a professional baseball player. When I was 17, I was selected for the US Olympic Junior baseball team. I then attended the University of Maryland on a baseball scholarship as a Finance major.

However, when I graduated, I didn't go into pro baseball after all. Not sure what to do, I decided to try my fortunes on Wall Street because I loved how Wall Street worked.

On Wall Street, you were as good as your profit and loss. Everything was based on your performance and focused on R E S U L T S! As long as you were successful, no one could tell you how good or bad you were. There was that freedom from judgment and your reputation was based on your performance. That was what got me into the business world, and I did that for about five years.

After that, I entered the marketing world and started learning about direct response marketing. I was amazed by the internet and how you could communicate with people all around the world 24/7 and make a lot of money. Because I was working online, which was already booming, I can remember taking a look at my computer and being excited about the opportunities in front of me.

As time went on, I did a few marketing jobs here and there, bouncing around a bunch. I couldn't stay put at a firm for too long because I wasn't satisfied. I got into a pattern where, having been at a job for a while making a few bucks, I would realize it was not what I wanted, and I'd take another job to see if it might be the one. I just couldn't find what I wanted to do and I wasn't getting paid the amount I wanted.

I've always had the entrepreneurial fire and nothing was going to be good enough until I was on my own. But frankly, I'd get scared and insecure about starting my enterprise; I didn't know what to do and I didn't have any money to invest.

In January 2008, the company I was working for had gone under. I was left with a decision. Should I find a new job or take a shot on my own? It didn't take long to make the decision. I felt if I was ever going to take a shot, it was the time to go for it. I had a plan; I would model some other businesses doing well at that time. I was scared sh*tless, but at the same time, I was filled with so much excitement and opportunity to begin the journey of finally launching my own business in performance marketing. At that time I was making $150,000 a year so I divided that by twelve and told myself if I could make that much money per month, I would be okay. My daughter was three, my son was a newborn, and we had just purchased our first house. I remember exchanging looks with my wife. I'm the dreamer in the family. Ali is not a risk-taker at all, however, she stood by me 100% and supported me as we realized we were going to have more stress in our lives. I'm not sure if I ever told her this but reflecting on those days I don't think I would have been able to make it if it were not for her support and love. I'm so thankful for her - she is my rock.

A friend of mine who was already a business owner offered to loan me $50,000 to start my business. The way he talked about it, he made it seem like it was a piece of toilet paper. A few years earlier, my dad had given me $50k to start a business and it was a complete failure. My mom had passed away from melanoma two years earlier and my dad wasn't in a financial position to just throw money away. Understandably, then, I was hesitant to take my friend's offer. Ultimately I didn't take his $50k because I was determined to launch my business on my own.

And yet, as a father, I understand more than ever that my dad's loan to me indicated unconditional support and he'd give it again if I asked. I realize now I attribute a big part of my current success to my parents who always made me feel like I could do anything once I focused on it. What was powerful about them instilling that belief in me was that it gave me the strength and confidence to reach for new successes and not be afraid to fail.

As scary as it was, starting my business was both exciting

and thrilling for me. I loved every bit of it and doing it made me feel alive. Fortunately, direct response marketing is a cash flow positive business, which means the amount you get paid always exceeds the amount you spend. By getting some early deals, I built a cushion from which to pay bills and feel a bit more at ease. As a performance marketer, I get paid for driving a result; I get paid for every lead I generate for my advertisers and I get paid each time I drive a result for a client. I broker deals for generating leads and there is an agreement in place on how much I get paid per each lead generated. It works similarly to baseball and Wall Street - all that mattered was performance - and that's the reason I resonated with this business model. It's result-driven, get-paid-for-performance without any judgment. The potential gain is unlimited and the work involves hustling, finding the right partners, and being opportunistic. I was like a shark smelling blood in the water. I would see an opportunity to generate more cash flow and I would focus my time on making it work. Instead of spending money on a logo or website, I put all my energy into sales and marketing.

In the first six months, I hustled and did a lot of side consulting to keep my primary business afloat. I usually got between $5,000 - $10,000 per consulting job. Pretty soon, I made anywhere from $40k - $50k per month. It was crazy for me because within a few short months I had already made more than the $150k my former job would have paid me. Since then, I've cultivated the belief that if you are not pushing yourself into that place of discomfort you are not growing. Sadly, this is the pit a lot of people find themselves in; they tend to limit themselves to a zone of comfort and are afraid to fail. I'm gonna tell you a little secret - EVERYONE FAILS! Success is easy. It's the failures that build character and strength.

Since having my first child, I cultivated the habit of saving a percentage of my earnings. It freaks me out to have debt so I see my investments as preparation for a rainy day. I don't want my life decisions influenced in any way by a financial or an emotional crisis. Week after week, I take a percentage of my earnings and put it in a Vanguard 500 Fund for myself and the kids. But at the end of the day, it's not always about the money. Consulting was as miserable as it was profitable for me. I worked "one-on-one" with up to a dozen people at a time and I felt they were just sucking information out of me. It was overwhelming and I only did it to generate money to put into my primary business.

## FINALLY GETTING DOWN TO BUSINESS

After six months of consulting, I realized I couldn't take it anymore. I finally decided to focus solely on my primary business. At this stage, I had one employee and my business was doing well even though I wasn't dedicating 100% of my time to it. At this point, I was generating enough cash flow that I could stop consulting and focus 100% of my time growing my business. The moment I decided to go ALL IN and focus on my business, everything changed. As a result of dedicating myself solely to getting direct advertiser deals, we grew month over month, with every month making new all-time revenue high's.

In 2008, I had two main deals running simultaneously. One was in insurance and the other was in online education. I hustled and functioned almost as an extension of their marketing department - except I didn't get paid for marketing. I only got paid when I generated leads for them. As an affiliate marketer, your goal is to secure direct advertiser relationships that result in exclusive deals. When you get 'an exclusive,' marketers have to go through you, giving you a lot more leverage to get traffic from publishers and allowing you to charge much higher margins. Also as an affiliate marker, I don't own any products.

My job is to grow sales of my affiliate's products. Based on the leads I generated they sold between $500,000 to $700,000 monthly. At a 30% margin, their sales translated to earnings of $150K-$210k per month for me. It was starting to become fun - I loved it!

In 'media math' if I get paid $10 for every lead with a profit margin of 20%, then for every $10 I make I can spend up to $8 to generate the lead, with a profit of $2. When I generate 1000 leads, my profit is $2 X 1000, or $2000. When I generate 10,000 leads my profit is $20,000 but I also had to spend $80,000 in one month to generate the leads to begin with. But that's OK because all my deals were set up to pay on collected revenue. This is important; it means I only pay my partners who were driving the traffic when I got paid from my advertiser. Therefore, I always had a positive cash flow.

However, affiliate marketing is a fragile business. No deal lasts forever and eventually, they stop. I learned this the hard way during my first year. After getting the deals set up and running, I would constantly monitor the quality of traffic. I'd have to turn off traffic that wasn't converting, and when leads stopped coming in the door so did my revenue. Both deals went away around the same time and I felt sick to my stomach but it taught me a valuable lesson that stays with me today. Now I'm always filling the pipeline. I think of my business as a chair with six legs; if one breaks, it's not good, but the chair is still standing and can carry the weight while we work on fixing the issue.

I am naturally inquisitive and I'm always eager to see what's next. So, after I lost those deals, I listened to the signals coming from my body, my stomach aches, telling me I had no control over the business. Yes, I loved it, and I made mind-boggling amounts of money. However, from an asset perspective, my only asset was my hustle and that's not a viable exit strategy for any business. I listened to my gut and decided to start email list marketing.

Rather than generating traffic to my site by buying costly media, I decided to focus on creating relationships with partners. I identified partners with large email lists, I managed and monetized them, and then we split the profit after expenses. I missed out on the wild wild west of the world wide web that happened in the early 2000s; I had some buddies who made $60 to $100 million at that time! But in just a short time, I had about a million emails that I could monetize being posted to my database every day from various partners. The way it worked was my partner would have a form on the internet for a certain offer. The user would land on the form, sign up, agree to the 'privacy policy, terms and conditions' and give permission for my partner to share their email address with my firm, and for us to send marketing messages to their inbox. It felt amazing to have so much data and the ability to press send!

2008, my first full year in business, was the hardest part of building everything I have today. After making it through that first year, I proved to myself I'll never have to work for somebody again unless I want to do so. Over the last dozen years, I've learned that no matter what happens, I know I'll figure out how to generate revenue from something.

## EVOLVING INTO SOMETHING BETTER

Being an entrepreneurial dad is hard and I have sacrificed a lot for my family. I've spent hours upon hours to create a good life for us. The reward is that now I can spend time with them when and how I want. I believe this is your goal, too.

Years ago when I got started, I had buddies in their twenties who were making half a million dollars a year as traders on Wall Street. I remember envying them because I wasn't earning anywhere close to what they were earning. That seemed like a lot of money to me then. But you know what? 20 years later, my friends are still on Wall Street doing the same things, earning the same amount, and they can't take more than five days off in a year.

From my perspective, this is unacceptable. Success is about family and freedom for me. Yes, we all worry about making a living, but there should be the freedom to do what you love. Today, I've set myself up in a way I can make a living and do what I love at the same time. As for my buddies, their problem is a form of "golden handcuffs."

Think about it. Not many people get paid $500,000 annually, especially in today's economy. If you are miserable and hate your job but feel you are making too much money to quit, the price you have to pay is too high. You might as well be in prison. In retrospect, I believe it was a blessing in disguise that I was unsuccessful at my many jobs earlier in my life because otherwise, I might not have ventured into entrepreneurship. I never would have found performance-based marketing and then got into lead generation, affiliate marketing, and email list management, and ways to monetize website traffic.

Between 2008-2020, we generated over 50 million leads with over one billion 'clicks' resulting in more than $100 Million in revenue for our company and our clients. Throughout that time I've had the same team working for me and we are like family. I love them, but a few years back I noticed that something was missing for me.

All through the time I was building my business, I never really went on the internet and pumped out *my* brand. I didn't think it was relevant to my business and purpose until I started listening to Russell Brunson's Clickfunnels podcast. Russell is a nice guy who co-founded a company called Clickfunnels. He makes you feel like he is your best friend each time you listen to his podcast. He's just a good dude with good values and it's not about the huge amount of money he makes. What's great about him are the core values that guide how he lives his life and professional career, and that they trickle down to his entire organization and his community.

## LEARNING FROM OTHER EXPERTS

I believe the reason so many people go to Clickfunnels events is because of him. What I love about him is that he came from my world of performance marketing, but he also lives in the world of influencers, coaching, and digital information products. The genius of what he did is marrying these two fields together into something truly wonderful.

Let me explain how media arbitrage works. Before I do I need you to understand the difference between paid traffic and free traffic. The major difference is that with paid traffic you are leveraging someone else's traffic. Free traffic is when you can get an impression on your website without paying for a click. Typically this happens from you ranking organically in Google search results, or maybe you have a following in social media or a podcast that will drive traffic to your website without having to pay for that click. Paid traffic is when you are willing to pay for someone to click on your ad. It could be a keyword in Google, a display ad on someone else's site, or an email sent to someone else's database to drive traffic to your website. When that happens you pay for the click based on the agreement you made with the publisher.

Here's a quick example of how media arbitrage works. Let's say you have a client who installs home security systems. The home security advertiser is willing to pay $100 for every qualified lead you generate. The home security client has a $700 allowable to spend on every new home security installation they get. Therefore, for every seven leads I generate, one of those leads needs to convert into a new sale, meaning a new home security installation. So I buy clicks (these are 'paid clicks') driving traffic to a destination that qualifies users - they must own a home and want to install a new home security system. I will do this with an 'allowable' - or budget - of no more than $75 for every lead I generate. Because the advertiser pays $100 per lead, I will profit at least $25 for every lead generated. If I buy clicks on the Google search engine, bid for the phrase "new home security system" and pay $15 for every click, then I have to convert into a payable lead 20% of every five clicks Google sends me. I pay $75 for five clicks ($15 X 5), one of those clicks turns into a payable lead, so I get paid $100 from my advertiser and keep $25. My advertiser needs to convert one of every seven leads I send them into a new customer. When all the pieces align, everyone is profitable and it's a win/win.

In performance marketing or any business, customer data is your company's biggest asset. You can email the person, transfer them to a call center, text them, and direct them to an offer they can click if they are interested in your product. Combining the world of performance marketing with that of digital products is a brilliant way to bring people into your world and offer them value.

I believe there is something about me that can be a great lesson for you. My recommendation to anyone trying to build a business is to focus on creating relationships and model how people run their businesses. Learn how others do things. Find out how they invoice, negotiate deals, get paid, and more. Most people tend to focus on nice cars and properties but I'm always interested in how people got to where they are. I love watching entrepreneurs like Bill Gates and Mark Zuckerberg. I always want to know how they became who they are today.

If you take the time to read about these guys, you will see they used to be just like us. I know it sounds crazy to think we can be like them but we can. If you believe you can, it's always possible for the business to snowball, and things can start happening. People impose limits around their lives but you don't have to. Did you know the highest-grossing revenue product on Shark Tank is a sponge? Think about that. Simple innovation and idea generation can lead anywhere!

## JOINING THE MILLION DOLLAR CLUB

Listening to Russel Brunson and buying his products only made me curious. The more I listened, the more I wanted to understand his process. I had the opportunity to be part of his Inner Circle, a Mastermind group for a handful of business owners. For $50,000 we met twice! I joined Russell's Inner Circle on

Ali's birthday — April 10th. It turned out to be one of my best decisions. I am so thankful I did because if I hadn't, I would still be in that gray area where I didn't understand how experts sell information products. The mastermind fast-tracked my success by about a hundred times. The people I met are amazing and I got to realize that there's a whole other world of digital marketing.

I met people who were out to make an impact and build a legacy. And I learned to change my perspective about lead generation. The biggest takeaway came when I witnessed the impact Russell made on his followers by showing them how to leverage the internet to get their message out into the world to the people who needed it the most. I learned to see that my expertise in lead generation and digital marketing could make a difference in a person's life. I realized I could indirectly make an impact and change the world by showing experts how to find the people who needed their help the most. By doing so, I can make a connection between two people who can help each other, and that all stems from knowing how to generate leads and convert those leads into new customers.

For example, if there is someone helping people with alcohol issues, I can be the person who helps the alcohol expert find people who need their help. I learned to see that I can directly make an impact on people's lives by helping them find customers or products. That was the game-changer for me.

I learned to see that there are great people with products and services but they don't understand the online marketing world. They don't know how to generate leads and make connections. I bridge the gap between people who need services and the service providers; that's powerful!

Currently, I have a direct response marketing company: Universal Marketing Partners. We have three main revenue streams: lead generation, site monetization, and an affiliate network that we own made up of hundreds of publishers.

Additionally, I've been working on building a new survey platform called SurveyDetective™. It's on version 2.0 and I've been investing massive hours, dealing with UI and UX designers, getting the hype out, while still running my business.

## INNOVATING THE USE OF SURVEYS

SurveyDetective™ is a simple online DIY survey builder tool that helps businesses convert visitors into leads and leads into customers. SurveyDetective™ simplifies online marketing, by providing users with pre-built survey options that help you identify your target market and position your marketing message to the right target market at the right time. SurveyDetective™ was created so that entrepreneurs like you, who have zero tech skills, can easily build survey funnels to convert ice-cold leads into customers! Let me show you it works:

You start by surveying your audience asking the right questions that allow your audience to self-declare their skill set and tell you what their objections, fears, and insecurities are about your 'vehicle' - your offer. Based on the results of the MARKET RESEARCH survey, you split your market into smaller groups of people with similar needs and identifiable characteristics. You then TARGET each group with custom-tailored marketing messages, POSITIONING your offer differently for each MARKET SEGMENT.

When you create marketing messages that make the customer feel relatable, the person feels as if you customized the product just for them when in fact, all you did was split your target market into different groups enabling you to tailor specific messaging to break down each target market's objections and disbeliefs without ever changing your core product.

When you follow our framework, your effective CPM's (cost per 1000 impressions) will skyrocket, you will lower your costs, and you'll market to fewer people making a much higher return.

In the world of marketing, people make a lot of mistakes. The primary one is trying to sell to everybody in the same way. Most marketers have one marketing campaign with the same emails and landing pages for everyone. Experience has taught me this approach isn't successful. To sell effectively, you need to understand your audiences and find out what their major objections are to purchasing your products and services.

The second mistake people make is that they try to create several different core offers. Your core offer has to stay the same while you alter your messaging. Selling requires you to isolate each objection to your core offer, dial into it, and solve it. Creating multiple offers simply confuses your prospect.

Let's imagine you are a seller and you have a lemonade stand on a popular street. People will have different objections to purchasing your lemonade. The first person may have the objection that your lemonade looks weird. The second person may have the objection that your lemonade costs $1 and they don't have enough money. The third person may have the objection that they are worried your lemonade might be too sweet or it might give them a stomach ache. You don't deal with those three different roadblocks by creating different offers. You must understand their objections and address them specifically. This is where surveying provides a solution.

By surveying people, you'll be able to put them in different groups and customize your campaign massaging for each group. You will be able to adjust your messaging so that it overcomes each objection, increasing the chances of closing a purchase. However, if you start addressing objections your prospect doesn't have, you will be creating disconnection and you won't be able to close a sale.

This is how I can help people fast track their business and help them avoid the tough issues that I went through. Experience has taught me some very valuable skills and practices. In affiliate marketing, as I get offers, I always make sure I understand those offers. I look at the objections so that I can create different groups for different marketing messages.

Take the scenario in which I send emails to a list of one million people about an insurance offer. Normally, if I'm lucky I might get a 1% click rate (10,000 people open the email) and 5% sales on those clicks (500 total purchases.) Remember that gathering a million emails will cost me a lot of money. And I also bought advertisements on Facebook and Google. So, there's a lot of investment at stake. If I get low click rates that will hurt my profit. However, if I can use surveys to carve off different groups of people and market to those people based on their specific needs, my offer is going to be more relevant, my click and conversion rates will be higher, and my profits will go up.

## BECOMING A SURVEYDETECTIVE™

My wish is to help people become survey detectives. I want you to understand that by becoming a survey detective, you will be able to go into the market and generate more leads than the majority of people in the information product world. Success comes from reaching more people and converting cold leads. Most people use surveys to get feedback and ask their customers and employees how satisfied they are - that's playing defense. However, I am positioning my platform as a detective. It's the only survey platform in the world with its main focus designed for generating leads for businesses- and that's playing offense.

Surveys are effective for various reasons: they allow you to segment and customize your messaging for different people; they allow you to focus on specific problems your customers have, and they allow you to have a process for your goals. Let's say you have a masterclass training that you want to sell. Your survey goal is to get people to register for your webinar. You want to follow the A.C.I.S.T.P. framework. Which means the following. A = attract, get the person's attention. C = curious, get the person to start the survey by creating a curious hook, I = identify what group each person belongs in, and S = Segment the groups by different characteristics. Then you want to T = Target each segment by P = positioning your core offer as the custom solution to each of your target markets' unique objectives.

Surveys work so well because people love to learn something about themselves. It's all about self-discovery. If a marketer wants to sell a copywriting product, they can create a survey that asks what five mistakes every copywriter makes. A leadership product can ask people about their leadership styles.

The most popular questions revolve around personality. Surveys can be applied to any niche. Assuming you are surveying e-commerce products, you can ask which camera is best for their business or which copywriting style is best for their email marketing strategy. By having this valuable information, you will be able to recommend the best fit for their situation. It's very cost-effective and the cost per lead that you are going to generate using a survey is less than that of conventional advertising; you can reduce your cost of generating a lead from $2 to as little as 50 cents because the conversion rate of the survey is higher.

That high rate is due to engagement. By getting people to click your survey, they have self-declared their problems to you. You are not guessing - they are telling you, "This is my issue - fix it." Additionally, you are pixeling the survey taker so that you can retarget them on Facebook without capturing their email address or name. This is a massive advantage and advanced marketing stuff. But anybody who understands Facebook retargeting knows how gigantic it is. If ten thousand people answer your survey and you convert half, you can still market to all of them via retargeting by pixeling them while being specific to how they responded to each question. These are just some of the advantages of surveys.

Another advantage is that Facebook won't shut down surveys the way it disapproves of your ad. Surveys help you meet people where they are today and you give them what they want and you make them curious and sell them what they need.

## BREAKING DOWN THE CONVENTIONAL BARRIERS

Surveys generate cold leads and this is their true power. Cold leads are people who have never heard about you or your business. Your ad is a pattern interruption to them and they need to get to know, like, and trust you a bit. Surveys help you build authority. Warm leads are those who have heard about you. They probably read your blog or they have signed up on a list, but they haven't purchased anything from you. Lastly, hot leads are those who have bought things from you or are likely to buy again.

I want you to understand that anyone can use SurveyDetective™. You can be someone who sells a product or service, you could promote someone else's offer, or you could generate leads for a client. Let's say you need leads specific to people who want to start a podcast. We could create a survey with a hook such as, "What's your podcast type?" You learn about the person and help them learn about themselves and what type of podcast they should start. At the same time, you are getting email data and building a list. Now, you own a list of people interested in becoming a podcast host and there's a lot you can do with those people. You can learn about them, sell to them right away, and start building your business.

This is the whole idea of the SurveyDetective™. The platform is meant for two sets of people. On one side are the influencers, experts, and producers with their info-products. These people need leads because they have something to sell. On the other side are the Certified SurveyDetectives™ who have gone through my training and understand how to use the survey tools to generate leads for people in the lead gen business. The goal is to certify some people as survey detectives so that if producers come to the platform and they don't have the time to learn how it works they can turn to people who are certified.

I envision it to be similar to what I did in my first businesses. Both parties will make money. Back then, I generated revenue for both the insurance and education offers by getting them leads. They paid me on a cost per lead basis for the leads. The point of SurveyDetective is to give people the ability to start their own business without having to learn everything.

However, you can create constant cash flow for your business with this platform once it launches. You have other people taking your offers, taking surveys, and the leads keep coming in. Even if you have events, you will be generating revenue until you have the events and then rake in your millions. And that's the point, isn't it? Because every business needs leads.

Eric

# James Golden

## WHAT ARE YOU WORKING FOR?

*James Golden, Founder and CEO of Pavement Management Group,
PMG, and Chief Action Officer of JG3 Consulting (JG3)
www.pavementmanagement.com
www.jg3consulting.com*

*"Some people want it to happen, some wish it would happen, others make it happen."*

Michael Jordan

*"Dream big, work hard, become legendary."*

James Golden

I'm currently 42 years old, and a father, a husband, and an entrepreneur. It's hard to believe I'm about to celebrate ten years as a business owner. When I reflect on my journey, I see it's been a wild ride, and one of progressing from "Good to Goalden." This phrase is a pun on my name, and I started using it within the last year to help propel me forward on my journey.

To guide you on your entrepreneurial journey, I would love to share with you pivotal moments of my journey.

The reality is that if you choose to enter the world of small business, you're probably already a high performer. Yet you have to realize that what got you into this space probably won't get you where you want to go. An entrepreneur's journey is about constant auditing. You have to keep reviewing and re-examining yourself, and changing as you go along.

Entrepreneurship is not your regular 9-to-5, punch-the-clock type of situation. It becomes even harder to navigate when you have family involved. This is because you will find yourself in a situation where everyone needs you. Your spouse and your kids need you, and at the same time, your business and employees need you.

I grew up in a lower-middle-class family. My dad had a job, and my mom was a stay-at-home parent with my brother and me. As a middle schooler, I grew up having Michael Jordan and Bo Jackson as my idols. They were the ones who had done things I wanted to do, and I wanted to be like them.

I wanted all the cool branded Nike stuff that helped you fit in with the crowd. But I knew it wasn't going to happen by magic. When I was growing up, we didn't go to chains and name-brand stores. We shopped at thrift and outlet stores. I realized real quickly that if I wanted to get those branded Jordans and Bo Jacksons, I had to work for them. It was that simple.

Because I knew I had to work for a living, entrepreneurship became the way out for me. I knew that no one else was going to provide for me. At a very young age, I understood what the business of making money was all about. I started by mowing lawns around the neighborhood. I would simply knock on my neighbor's door and then I would say, "Hey, can I mow your lawn?" They'd respond, "Absolutely," and I would earn $20 bucks. Then, after I was done, I'd be off to the next neighbor.

Soon I was making $80 per week mowing grass in the summer. Back in the early nineties, trading baseball cards, football cards, and things like that was a popular activity, so I got into that, too. I was usually at the mall, and I was stacking and selling these things and making a good profit on investments as a kid.

That's just the first part of my story as a kid. The second part began when I took over a paper route business from a friend who was going on a vacation. Back in those days, we didn't have what the kids nowadays have. There was no Internet, and newspapers were printed every day. Newspaper companies distributed their product the way they always had; they trusted twelve-year-old kids like me to handle all aspects of the paper route distribution.

The papers were dropped off in sections, and I had to put everything together. I had to create a system to knock on doors to collect payments, and I had to figure out a distribution process that got the papers to the right customers. It was crazy, but as a kid navigating life, I knew no better, and I just had to figure it out. I've since come to realize that's what got me systematized as a person. Since then, I have learned not to rely on a micromanager or a boss to tell me what to do.

## LEARNING TO FIGURE THINGS OUT ON MY OWN

At age 19, I found myself being that guy coming out of high school who had gotten his girlfriend pregnant. She was a year younger than me and she was the one I took to prom. Coming out of high school, we were that pregnant couple. I enrolled at a local technical college, and I was considering drafting design technology as a good career option.

With my girlfriend pregnant and still considering what to do with my future, an opportunity opened up; I was introduced to a family friend who was starting a pavement management and consulting company. The man was willing to pay me $10 an hour, and my job was very simple. All I had to do was drive around all day, get in and out of the car, walk down roadways, and document the different types of cracks, distresses, and every other problem in the road surface. Then I had to file everything and present it to my boss.

That was how I was out on the road every day all by myself with no boss. I had to rely on myself to get things done. When you think about this, it's difficult. It's difficult to get up every day, exercise, eat breakfast, and to take on all the responsibility that comes with being a parent and a business owner.

As a young man with a pregnant girlfriend, navigating how to become a father and dealing with marriage, I had to be very goal-oriented. I had to start setting up my day for success. I had to rely on myself and hold myself accountable.

The company I worked with was a startup in the engineering space. My mentor trusted me to always get the job done. He only gave me some light metrics and I had to figure out my processes and systems to get things done. Just as I had done when I was a paperboy, I had to rely on my own sales distribution skills.

In 1999, we didn't have zoom calls, and neither did we have apps, phones, or email the way it is today. As employees, we had to meet at places like Tim Hortons and Bob Evans to have a physical meeting to review business.

Back then, the entrepreneur in me was always asking questions. I wanted to know more about why I was collecting the data and what my boss was doing with the data. I kept asking myself, "What's the impact of the data I'm gathering? Is there a system it's going into?" I was always asking my mentor at work, and myself, these questions every step of the way.

Eventually, I worked at the company for 13 years, from the age of 19 until I was 32. All through that time, I'd been leveling-up; I even went back to college, did it all online while working full time, earning a bachelor's degree in information technology. At work, I also started learning more, and building teams and systems around what I was doing. Eventually, I became the Director of Operations. At the same time, we continued to grow our family, and during those 13 years, my wife and I had two more children, built our second home, and we're enjoying the classic American Dream. Or so we thought.

## NAVIGATING DIFFICULT CIRCUMSTANCES AND MAKING BIG DECISIONS

When we first discovered we were having our first kid as kids ourselves, we started life out together by renting space in my parent's basement. We were grateful for the option, but getting out on our own quickly became the mission. After a long two years, and at 20 and 21 years old, we were able to build our first home. There we were, two kids with a child, a mortgage, car payments just trying to navigate life together. The massive amount of responsibilities at such a young age would prove to be both a detriment and a blessing.

Back then, credit cards were simple and straightforward. If you had a job, you could get a credit card. Looking back, I think that was one of the things that complicated our problems. We were paying the bills, but at the same time, we were racking up credit card debt. The fact that we didn't understand life or finances took a heavy toll on our marriage and our kids.

Unfortunately, things only got worse. Three days after

Christmas in 2010, I got a call from my boss asking for a meet-up at the corporate headquarters. That's when my boss told me that he was "closing the doors on the business." He had decided it was in his best interest at the time to semi-retire. The plan was to wrap up our existing projects over the next 3 months, solo. All employees except myself were let go, but because of our relationship, he had decided to allow me to handle things solo over that period to retain health insurance and a paycheck for myself and family while affording me a window of time to determine what would be next for my career.

And that was how my life changed in an instant. I was shocked and I didn't understand what was happening. I had many questions at that moment, but I couldn't ask them. People who know me will tell you that I'm a pretty strong human being. But that day, I walked out of that office, got into my car, and felt the weight of the world on my shoulders, broke down and cried for probably the first time in my life.

Even though we were struggling with life, it was about to get a lot harder. I picked up my cell phone and made the difficult call to let my wife know what was happening. She needed to know that within the next couple of months I'd be without a paycheck, without health insurance, and in a rough spot to make this mortgage, car, and credit payments. That moment was pivotal in my life because I realized that I only had two choices: I could either go figure out a new career path and go get a new job, or I could start my own company.

After that call, I spent the next 45 minutes driving home, with a face full of tears, full of anxiety and worry. I was 32 years old, making $75,000 a year, carrying $35,000 in debt, with my marriage on the rocks, three kids to support, and I was about to lose my job. Starting my own company was something I'd always had at the back of my mind because of my life experiences mowing lawns, selling baseball cards, as a paperboy, and as an entrepreneur for the past 10 years.

I had to ask the question, "What do I do?"

One of my favorite quotes is from Michael Jordan and it became my mantra from that day forward. "Some people want it to happen, some wish it would happen, others make it happen." This quote helped to lay the foundation necessary for me heading down the road of personal growth and development.

The beginning of 2011 was rough. The end date to a paycheck and health insurance was creeping closer and our marriage was nothing short of on the rocks. My wife understood, and to her credit, saw earlier than I did that we had no future together. She was ready and prepared to move on while I was too focused on the financial downfall that comes with divorce, while now starting my own business. I found myself in a dark place. I lost my job, my marriage dissolved, she and the kids moved out, and here I was living alone in the house we had built together and trying to navigate the start of my new company. I transitioned from being a married and working individual to being a solopreneur who was now always on the road and starting life all over again at 32 years old.

The day I went to finalize the divorce in court was also the day I met a sheriff outside. He handed me the foreclosure papers for my home. Then, I had to short sell and move out of the house. I was very blessed back then to have a strong relationship with a realtor who was able to take care of the situation before the house foreclosed on me.

That was how I found myself, at the age of 32, back living in my parents' basement. I had bills to pay and I had to take care of my ex-wife and the three kids. I was just trying to wrap my head around what the hell had just happened. My life had changed almost in an instant, so hopes and dreams were not a priority back then. The number one priority was figuring out how to get out of bed the next day. I had to pull myself up from the bootstraps and get up every day to get the job done.

No one was going to give me any cash, and it took me a couple of months to finally figure out a direction. That direction came about after I got into personal development and after I met someone. It's interesting what happens when you start focusing on yourself and you go down the road of personal development.

I went on Facebook for the first time, and I struck up a conversation with a woman I had dated in high school. I was just trying to rekindle the relationship I had with her. I had no clue that she was the one who was going to come and rescue me and help build me further.

That was how I met Jamie, who has now been my wife for six years.

I was already into personal development when I met her but she helped paint a vision of the future for me. She helped show me what the right partner can be and how to bring my three kids and her two kids to have one big happy family. It's hard and difficult to navigate our big family because we are like a crazy bunch. We've been able to do it successfully and persevere because of the vision of the future we painted.

We have been able to work together on core family values and we kept leveling each other up. With her help, I've also got a great relationship with my ex-wife and we've been able to co-parent just fine.

## TAKING ACCOUNTABILITY FOR YOUR ACTIONS

During those difficult times, I started developing new mindsets. I learned to come out of the anger I was accustomed to all those years and to figure out why life had handed those circumstances to me as a young man. Looking back, I don't think I took enough accountability for my actions. It took being stripped down to the bare bones and then having my current wife come into the picture before I could get to where I am now.

I've been a business owner for the last ten years and I made a huge pivot to take my business where it is today. I've learned a lot of things along the way. I've learned to audit constantly. I've developed the habit of looking at what's happening in the market, and the needs of my clients, and that of my family quarterly. Because at times, it's all about auditing yourself and being able to have difficult conversations with your spouse, kids, clients, employees, and business partners.

During my darkest days, I adopted Michael Jordan's mantra

of dreaming big, taking action, and becoming legendary. As I mentioned earlier, I was very entrepreneurial as a kid, so I worked hard. I started my company, dreamed big, thought outside the box, and kept working to get the things I needed in my life.

I came to realize that success is about your work ethic and taking accountability. I realized that by taking action, I got what I wanted with my first marriage. So I decided to repeat it once more with my kids and with my business. But as the mantra goes, to become legendary you need to leave a legacy, and that legacy is different for everyone. Leaving a legacy is about asking the right questions. Why are you doing the things you are doing? What is it all going to be for? What are you trying to leave? What is that legacy for your family? What are you working for?

## BUILDING WITH THE FUTURE IN MIND

Currently, my wife and I are building our dream home, on a beautiful three-acre city lot that we are going to call the Golden Estate. Five years ago, the Golden Estate was our vision for the future. It's coming together today because we kept putting actionable plans behind the vision. The Golden Estate will be part of our legacy. We built it because we want it to be in the family for generations. The intention behind it is that our kids will have a place they can come back to when we're growing older. That's one of the legacies we want to leave behind.

We also have another legacy regarding our kids. Our legacy is that we want all our kids to understand life values, the things that come with life, and how to build up strong human beings. Being a dad and stepdad of boys and girls, all different ages, is certainly a daily challenge that comes with its ups and downs. Some relationships are harder than others but I've learned to be transparent, and open to the best of my abilities. With the help of Jamie, I've come to see that by being willing to work on myself and reach out for help, everything can be okay. It's also really great to have a good partner who always keeps me in check. She knows what to say and how to keep me on track, and I've been doing the same for her.

Building towards the future is also very exciting from the business perspective. Twenty years ago, I was a pavement inspector, walking around roadways all day, taking notes of distresses, and doing everything manually. Today, we're developing artificial intelligence, behind specific systems and processes to help streamline our entire company operation. Because we primarily work in the business-to-government space, our objective is to save taxpayer dollars by helping Public Works officials best manage the annual maintenance and repair of the roadways we all utilize each day.

This is how I've been able to leverage my life experiences, education, and unique skill sets to develop a meaningful career that I'm passionate about. I think there is a powerful message in this for you, especially those early on in their success journey. You have to realize that success is not a destination, rather a journey filled with detours, wrong turns, dead ends, and road-blocks. It's one of the key takeaways from my journey and is what has allowed me to continue pushing forward each day.

I've developed the habit of asking myself vital questions along my success journey. As a person into personal develop-ment, I wonder, "How can I be a better person tomorrow? What books can I read to improve my personal development?" And it's not different in business. In the business world, you either innovate or die.

If you think about the last few decades of business, you know that Blockbuster was a behemoth in the video rental space. Then, all of a sudden, a company called Netflix came and changed everything. They told everyone that instead of coming to the brick-and-mortar rental store, hoping to find what you wanted, they were going to ship movies to your house. Guess what? They won, and it's the same thing with Amazon and many others.

We are now having everything shipped to our doorsteps. At my company, we are also trying to do the same, and we work on automating the process of collecting the data. We are telling the story through charts, graphs, and videos. We are letting the councils and citizens who drive these roads every day understand that there is a process. You don't need a civil engineering degree anymore to understand what's happening with your roads. This is how we are trying to have more impact and do our part in pavement preservation.

Think about it. When you buy a car, you know you are going to wash that car and change the oil every few months and do the regular maintenance. The reason you do this is that you want to extend the life of your car. Unfortunately for America, we have not been doing that in terms of our infrastructure. We have not been providing proper preventative maintenance and preservation to our roadways.

At my company, Pavement Management Group, we are innovating the process of collecting the data so that there is information that our public works directors, city engineers, mayors, city council folks, as well as you, the taxpayer, can collectively have to make better and more timely decisions for the future improvement of all of our roadway networks.

## THE STORY OF BECOMING GOALDEN

As I said earlier, my favorite quote comes from Michael Jordan, "Some people want it to happen, some wish it would happen, and others just make it happen." Every time I read that quote, it gives me goosebumps. The key lesson in that quote is about taking action, and that has been massive for me.

Ten years ago taking action became a vital part of my journey. I determined to be a better version of myself every day. Because it has always stuck with me along my entire journey, one thing I want you to take away is that imperfect action always wins out over no action.

This is an idea that I make sure all my kids understand. As a kid, we dreaded thinking about the big ugly word, "failure." Nobody wants to fail so we all grow up worried about failing. No one wants to go in front of his or her peers and try something and then fail to succeed. We all grow up too worried about what others think about us.

This is not good for us because having that fear holds us back from taking action. Let me tell you a quick story. Imagine you went out with your buddies and you were having a great time. The next thing you knew, you had a revolutionary idea and shared it around the table. The idea might have been a product destined to be a market disruptor, a top service, or a better way of doing something. But rather than taking action on the idea, you simply talked about it.

The next thing you knew, two years passed. And as you turned up the TV you saw your idea. You realized that someone else had your same idea, but they took action and changed the world with it.

This happens all the time, and you may even start telling your friends that someone stole your idea. But that would be wrong. No one stole your idea. I want you to understand that. You made the choice not to work on the idea and patent it.

This is what you need to realize. By taking imperfect action, you will be moving in the right direction. You may take two steps forward and one step back, but it's okay as long as you move forward. This is what "failing forward" means. When I look back on my journey, I know that I took imperfect action. I had to bet on myself, step outside of my comfort zone, and just do whatever was necessary to move forward.

## CHANGING YOUR GOAL SETTING PERSPECTIVE

I recently launched a group called The Goalden Collective. The group is for like-minded high performers committed to living by the Golden Rule while taking action on their unique goals and dreams.

I have friends right now who are 42 years old and they still make the same amount of money and still live in the same house they did a decade ago. They still drive the same cars they did when they were younger. If they were content I wouldn't be concerned. I would be happy for them. But these friends of mine are each living a life of regret. They're living a life of sorrow because they never bet on themselves, nor did they take the actions necessary to level themselves up.

Sometimes, it's as simple as putting yourself out there, getting uncomfortable, and being willing to risk failure. It's as simple as that. The Goalden Collective was something I struggled with for about two years. I was worried about how the entrepreneur space was going to react to a pavement management expert who wanted to talk about personal development. I had to dig deep again and realize that I simply needed to start, to take the actions necessary to get it done.

The next thing for you to consider is how to set goals. While it's okay to take imperfect action, you want to make sure that you're setting goals every step of the way. It doesn't matter whether your goal is within your relationship, business, or with your clients. You want to make sure you are setting goals for yourself.

So what is a goal? A goal is the object of a person's ambition or effort. Think about a goal in soccer. The ball doesn't magically go through the hands of the goalkeeper. It takes a whole series of efforts and imperfect actions to get the ball to hit the back of the net.

Setting goals is not a problem. Anybody can set a goal. On the 31st of December every year, millions of people set New Year's resolutions. But we all know that only a few will eventually stick with them.

Why? The reason behind that is because most people's goals are not SMART. A SMART goal is an acronym for a goal that is Specific, Measurable, Attainable, Relevant, and Time-based. SMART goals are the way to level up. If your New Year's resolution is "to lose some weight," it's probably not going to happen. It's much too vague.

Recently, I lost 20 pounds within 75 days by committing to completing the 75 Hard Challenge from my mentor Andy Frisella. You can learn all of the details of the challenge by visiting https://andyfrisella.com/pages/75hard-info.

Beginning August 1st, 2020, I committed to doing the following every day, for 75 consecutive days:

- Take a daily progress picture

- Read 10 pages from a personal development book

- A 45-minute indoor workout

- A 45-minute outside workout

- Drinking one gallon of water

- Sticking to a meal plan with no sweets, cheat meals, or cheat days

- Drinking no alcohol

The beauty of this challenge is also the most difficult… choice.

You are free to choose the meal plan, books to read, and workout program to follow. This requires the next-level mental toughness, and discipline to overcome those objections we all find ourselves using. To ensure success I had to establish my own SMART goals over the 75 days, and leveraged my daily Google Calendar to schedule my workouts and activities as well as an app called Lose It! that I used to track my food, calories, and exercises.

Also, after finding a way to measure my progress, I had to make sure the goal was time based and realistic. If I simply had said I wanted to lose 20 pounds in 20 days, that was not going to happen, and would even be dangerous. However, I knew I could accomplish it in 75 days because that was a realistic timeframe.

Lastly, the goal needed to be relevant, or else I was going to quit early. Fortunately, being physically fit and healthy was relevant to my goals moving forward. It's always been relevant to me because I want to set a good example for my kids.

You want to make sure that your goals are SMART and they have all these attributes. You can't just think you want to lose weight this year. That goal is not SMART because 'this year' is not time-based. SMART goals are very important. Again, they stand for goals that are Specific, Measurable, Attainable, Relevant, and Time-based.

The two major concepts that I want you to remember from

this section are "taking action" and "setting SMART goals." You may be struggling with something right now. It may be finding clients, something that has to do with your kids or a matter in a personal relationship. The takeaway is to realize that you are not perfect and you don't ever need to chase perfection.

Start setting some SMART goals and then follow through with as much action as you can. Be willing to step out of your comfort zone and take imperfect actions to reach your next level. These are the things that have helped me all through my life. If these two things resonate with you right now, you can come on in and join my free Facebook group, The Goalden Collective. It's all about leveling each other up through action-based goal setting. We'd love to have you!

## DON'T SWEAT THE SMALL STUFF

As I reflect on the last two decades, I want to acknowledge the recession that began at the end of 2008 as well as the current Covid-19 pandemic. The harsh reality is that a lot of people have been affected by these situations, suffering job loss, loss of revenue, business failures, stress, and more.

The same thing happened to me three days after Christmas

in 2010. I was thrown into the deep end and I had to make the toughest decision of my life within 60 days. I didn't understand what the future looked like. I can remember taking those imperfect actions I talked about earlier. I jumped all in and the only thing I knew was that I had decided to start my own company.

Back then what I knew was that I had a skillset in pavement management and preservation. But that was not something that was lighting up the billboards in 2011. On top of that, the country was still in a recession and jobs were not plentiful. As I thought about this back then, I noticed that worries were creeping into my mind.

As I was thinking about all the exciting branding stuff and what I was going to name my company, the doubts also started creeping in. And then anxiety came with it. I started worrying that my regular paycheck was not going to show up, that my health insurance was going to run out. I started thinking that I had to figure out how to generate some revenue. I had to make money to pay the bills and to continue providing for my wife and the kids. On top of that, there was $35,000 in credit card debt that wasn't going away just because I had lost my job.

You may be in that type of situation today. You may be

going through what I went through back then - getting a phone call from corporate and finding out you just lost your job. It's very difficult to get through something like that and many of us are not prepared to handle such news. It's not surprising that there is so much depression and anxiety these days.

I also think one of the major reasons we struggle in our relationships is because we don't deal with these things very well. So, one simple lesson I learned the hard way was not to sweat the small stuff. This was an idea from a book with the same title, "Don't Sweat the Small Stuff" written by Richard Carlson.

Back in 2010, I was not yet on any personal development journey. But I remember I had the book lying somewhere around the house. My focus back then was always on tomorrow and how I was going to start generating revenue. My boss probably gave the book to me in the early 2000s, but I didn't read it. It was only after I started developing myself that I found the book. It's amazing what starts to enter your life when you begin to focus and use visualization as a daily tool.

The premise of the book lies in how we handle the daily challenges that come into our lives. Many people get upset when faced with challenges. But when you're on a mission to go from Good to Goalden, you have to push that to one side. You have to tell yourself that you cannot be sweating the small stuff. Because everything is small stuff!

Back to my story . . . when all those doubts started creeping into my mind, it started putting my mindset in a position of negativity. I was being led down a bad path. I was lucky to pick up that book and get the key takeaways. The biggest takeaway I got from the book is not to worry about what we can't control.

You can say, "James, losing your job - a career in such a specialized industry - and having a family, credit card debt, a mortgage, are not small, that's big stuff." You may think that, but at the end of the day, I learned that thinking that way was one of my problems. The key takeaway is learning to see that problems are lessons.

If you are having struggles right now, you need to start seeing that you need to understand those problems. You need to see that problems are not valid reasons to get worried or to start feeling sorry for yourself. You've got to start taking accountability for every problem that's at hand. This is what it takes to be a strong parent at home and a strong leader in your business. Tying the whole story together, I had to see that what was happening to me was an opportunity.

I like to call it a "Goalden Opportunity". I started to see that losing my job was a driving force and that now was the time to start that business of mine. Yes, I was worried about everything — income, revenues, paying bills, paying for food, and putting clothes on the backs of my family members.

I started to see that those are trivial things.

If you take a good look at my situation, at the end of the day, I could easily have gotten another paycheck job. Yes, even though it was 2011 and the nation was coming out of a recession, if I had to get a job, I could go get it. If that didn't work out, I could always work at Wendy's, or I could go deliver pizzas. Back then, a lot of people did just that, and there are so many inspiring stories that came out of that recession.

I had to see that losing my job was not happening to me, it was happening for me. This allowed me to plant my roots fully into entrepreneurship. I began seeing that this was what I was born to do.

Currently, my pavement management consulting business is firing on all cylinders and our clients are enjoying the fruits of all the hard work because I didn't give up back then. I saw my difficult circumstance as an opportunity to refocus and re-engage in important activities.

Ed Mylett, a mentor of mine always says, "Things happen for you, not to you." Now when you think about that for a second, that quote suggests opportunity. Thinking about that time, it was one of the things that guided me. I was always asking how to reposition my mindset from negative to an abundance and growth mindset.

I was able to get out of that situation because I stopped sweating the small stuff. I knew there was probably a plan out there and that if I kept thinking positively and taking one step after the other, things were going to go right for me. To be real, I didn't have it all figured out all at once. I still found myself occasionally at the bar, drinking whiskey to drown my sorrows. Then, my mindset hadn't shifted. But I had to get through that period. I had to go through those dark times when I was all alone before I could get to where I am now.

## MAKING USE OF WHAT THE WORLD THROWS AT YOU

Back in 2011, I was unaware of the whole personal development industry. It didn't exist in my grand scheme of things. I was not a person who was fully active online. I was not on Facebook. I had a core group of friends that I developed through marriage and high school. But due to the divorce, many of those relationships were suddenly stripped away. The divorce brought things into perspective and I realized that my friends had to make tough decisions. But because I didn't want to bring a me-versus-my-wife situation to all my friends I chose to lock myself away, start over, and go down the road of self-discovery. I decided not to sweat the small stuff.

I traveled five days a week for work, and I knew I wasn't going to see my kids every day because of the divorce. I was on the road doing pavement assessments and working late on reports for my clients. At first, I couldn't believe what was happening to me. But I learned to cope and to see the opportunity in the hardship. I started to see that I couldn't take things for granted and that I shouldn't sweat the small stuff.

I had to figure out how to get closer to my kids. There was a one-year-old, a ten-year-old, and a thirteen-year-old. They had all these different needs, from soccer and guitar to dealing with the baby. I was able to bond with the one-year-old but the others wanted to play with their friends. I had to adjust to all of that.

Also, I had to figure out how to start a business. I started thinking that if I kept pushing forward every day, something positive was going to come out of it. Those positives became tenfold when I started adopting an abundance mindset. I became truly grateful for where I was in life and I stopped worrying about the things I couldn't control. I stopped being worried about what people said about me.

Since then, all I have wanted to do was to take the imperfect actions necessary to develop myself as a human being. I recognized that I was no longer a 19-year-old kid but a 32-year-old adult who started a company. Now, I'm excited to say that I'm a 42-year-old father, husband, and entrepreneur, finally on the road to becoming Goalden, and fulfilling my legacy.

James

## Cody Loughlin

WHAT ARE YOU GOING TO DO ABOUT IT?

*Cody Loughlin, Founder of TheMoneyTalkers.com*
*Host of Money Talkers Podcast*

*"You Can't Build A Reputation On What You Are Going To Do."*
Henry Ford

*"You Are The Only Person Who Can Make Yourself Happy."*
Linda Loughlin

It all began in my first finance class at the University of Central Florida. Up until that point, I had little knowledge of money. But I had grown up in an entrepreneurial home and I've always felt that I could open a business if I wanted to. I never grew up with any limiting beliefs that I couldn't succeed in business.

I played three sports in high school, and I grew up close to my dad. He was the type of dad who never missed a practice or game. He was always there watching and cheering me on, even to my embarrassment at times. As you can imagine, it was difficult losing him when I was just 19 years old. His death tossed my life upside down.

I got into college with Marine Biology as my major. But I was still searching for direction when, in that fateful finance class, I stumbled upon the concept of compound interest. There I was, in the class listening to the professor as he explained how every kid in America could become a millionaire with very little effort or money.

It was mind-blowing for me because this was an idea I once thought to be impossible. I can remember being super happy at having the opportunity to learn this concept. However, as I understood more about it, that happiness transformed into anger. I thought about the kids with whom I had played sports in high school and the massive disadvantage they had. Most of them would never go beyond high school, and maybe 30 percent would make it to a United States college. I didn't know how many eventually got into a finance class or how many would eventually learn what I was learning.

I got angry because I had not been introduced to this concept until I was in college. It was infuriating thinking about all the boring classes and useless information that had been crammed into my head. I had a lot of information such as calculus that I was never going to use, and meanwhile, I had no idea what compound interest was, even though this was a subject that was going to affect me for life. Because I've always been a numbers person, I was captivated by this. This is the reason I later switched to a finance degree.

In a few years, I began telling my friends that I was going to be a millionaire by the age of thirty. As you can imagine, half of them laughed at me. However, some people believed me, and they asked how I was going to do it. The truth back then was that I had no idea how I was going to do it! I only knew I was going to do it. This is because I never believed for a moment that you couldn't do things like that. I grew up believing that if somebody could do it, I only had to figure out how.

It was as a result of this belief that at the age of 24 years, I opened my first company.

## MY FIRST MAJOR SUCCESS AND DOWNFALL

My first company was a mortgage company but I opened it without a great business plan, and I had only enough initial capital to keep the doors open for a month. It was a hell of a mess. We started with five people and rotated one phone among ourselves. Everything we did was on that same phone, and we had mix-and-match chairs that cost $10 apiece.

However, it was fun, and we had a lot of hustle. Within two years, I had started four other companies, and the mortgage company alone was doing a million dollars a year in commissions, with over 30 employees in a half-million-dollar condo by the beach. Everything was working perfectly until the tide suddenly ran out. I made the mistake of living too luxuriously, and within six months, I was broke. I had $700,000 in debt, with nowhere to live, no job prospects, and zero businesses. I owed money to the IRS; I hadn't filed taxes in two years and I had eight tax returns to file. It was a nightmare.

The only bit of luck I had was that I had credit cards that weren't canceled immediately. It was an unbelievable situation that made me sad for a while. And yet, one thing that helped was the mentality I had instilled in myself from when I was a kid who was taking ownership. I knew I had to take ownership of what happened. As a human, we are all allowed to feel self-pity, but never for too long. In this life, you have to get better if you want to win.

Randomly, I next decided to become a commercial banker. The real reason behind this decision was that I knew I could make money doing business. However, I also knew that I lacked the proper experience required to successfully run a business, as evidenced by my prior disasters.

I went after the banker's job because I knew I would be dealing with business owners. I believed I would get exposed to the habits of business owners—both the successful ones and the lousy ones—and be able to figure out how to properly build a successful business once again. That was why I got busy building my resume and went down to Wachovia.

There I was, a 28-year-old who had built four million-dollar companies from scratch, entirely self-taught. I listed my successes and I can tell you it felt really good preparing that resume. I proceeded to get three letters of recommendation and I sent out 25 applications within an hour.

If only life were that easy, right? I was crushed when 24 applications came back declined. It was another unbelievable experience because I thought that with my huge credentials anyone would be crazy not to want me. To make matters worse, I eventually got one phone call, but it wasn't what I was expecting. It was for a job paying $24,000 a year in Florida. When I told the lady on the phone I thought her call was a mistake, she simply said, "Oh, okay, well good. You answered so I can check it off." When I asked what she meant, she replied that they weren't really looking to hire me and that she was only calling because she didn't have enough people to call.

That was when I decided to flip the conversation. I said to her, "You're going to talk to me."

"Excuse me?" she said.

"Yes, you are going to talk to me because I need to talk to you."

She told me I was a mortgage person and that they were not hiring from my industry. I told her I didn't want her job but I did want the business banker job. I remember hearing her laugh after I said that.

We later had a polite conversation together, and she told me that I was overqualified for the job. But I didn't allow that to stop me. I asked her to connect me to the recruiter for the business banking position. She told me they weren't going to hire me. But I replied that I wasn't looking to get hired—all I wanted was an interview.

She was able to include me in the email. So, after waiting for two days with no call, I started emailing the recruiter. Four days later, the recruiter finally called me and asked me to stop, but I replied that the only way I was going to stop was if I got my interview. She reiterated it would be a waste of my time; I insisted I was only looking for a chance. And that was how I got my first interview.

## A LESSON IN INTENTIONALITY

Before I drove to Fort Myers for the interview, I prepared seven pages of notes and a business plan. I had 30-, 60-, and 90-day marketing plans prepared. All this was stuff I had done for marketing in my previous businesses. I went there wearing the only suit I had, and with a really bad pair of shoes. As I got there, I saw four guys immaculately dressed in expensive suits, wristwatches, and briefcases.

They were each over 45 years old, while I was just twenty-eight. I knew I wasn't going to stick out with my looks, my resume, or my experience. I had never been in a job interview before, because immediately after I got out of college, I had become a mortgage broker. So, I had to think about what I had that those guys didn't and where I could beat them.

The interviewers asked situational questions and they wrote down each candidate's answers. I quickly listed out to the interviewers the things I had that the other guys didn't.

I told them I had more hustle.

I had no bad habits, and I sold that as hard as I could.

I told them I was a problem solver.

I promised to outwork and outpace anyone they could put in the position.

I showed them my extensive notes and business plans.

They thanked me politely and said they'd call me in a couple of weeks if they had something for me.

As I drove home, I called my wife and informed her about everything. After that, I decided to take a break by visiting a friend. I can remember we were sitting by the fishing pond about an hour later and my phone rang. To my surprise, it was the recruiter; she was calling about the job.

She bluntly stated they didn't know if they could afford me! She wanted to know what salary I was hoping for. I had done a bit of research on possible salary ranges so told her a figure at the high-end of the range…. She promised to call me back.

Five minutes later, she called and offered me the job. If you have a job, you'll know how good it feels to get an offer. I moved my family down to Sarasota and started three days later.

Two to three months into the job, when all the banks were crashing, the manager came over and said to me, "Just so you know, there are 14 people on the team now and there won't be 14 people at the end of the year." He told me that I was the last to get hired, plus the youngest and that I had negotiated the highest salary. He made me realize I had the odds stacked against me.

I emphasized to him that he had no idea what I had gone through to get hired and wasn't about to give up now, so I asked what he suggested. He was by far the best manager I've ever had because when I asked him what to do, he told me to make myself "unfireable."

He told me I couldn't simply compete—I had to destroy the competition. So I decided to make myself indispensable. When my colleagues were busy making 20 phone calls and a couple of appointments a week, I was doing 80 to 120 calls a day and booking 8 to 10 appointments a day. Mind you, I had no connections and these people had been in banking for decades and relied on their connections.

Since I didn't have a ready-made network I chose to pursue businesses and had identified about 300 businesses that were qualified to work with me. I felt bad for some as I had so recently been in their shoes, having to deliver a loan that would take them out of business. This was where I started to see patterns and got to learn what distinguished a good business owner from a bad one.

At the end of that year, I was one of just seven people left. Because I refused to let them fire me I outworked everyone. For the next two years, I was number one on the team. I also became the number one loan producer on the west coast of Florida, closing $4 million in loans and delivering roughly $48 million in loan applications.

During that time, I got to realize how bad I was at managing money. I realized every failure I had suffered was entirely my fault. I had always believed I was a wizard with money, but now I could see I wasn't. That realization led me to listen to CDs by Dave Ramsey. I stopped watching TV entirely and submerged myself in financial information.

## TAKING RESPONSIBILITY AND LEVERAGING YOUR RESOURCEFULNESS

As I was straightening my life out, I decided to work on my debts, too. I can remember taking my eight unfiled tax returns to an accountant. It represented an incredible amount of work because the accountant had to reconstruct data from the few bank accounts and statements I had kept. He originally quoted me $1,500 per tax return, but I told him I didn't even have $500. In true entrepreneurial fashion, I started thinking about how to make a bargain with the resources I had.

I knew I needed his help so I negotiated; I promised to refer my business connections to him in exchange for his discounted services. He agreed to do all eight returns for just $800 total and told me to come back in a month. When he finished, he said I owed $27,000 to the IRS. I was ecstatic because I thought I owed more. For the next 30 days, everything was amazing! I was closing deals left and right because I was so happy. But a nasty surprise was waiting because I'd been correct about owing more, much more. The IRS notified me that I owed not $27,000 but $98,000.

Can you imagine putting a pin to a balloon right now? My

world exploded because I had no idea how to come up with that much money. But then my wife asked the critical question, "What are you going to do about it?"

This mindset shift is essential because there is a timeframe between being upset about a situation and then determining what to do about it. The fact is, you are always going to have to handle a situation at some point. It's simply a matter of choice. Will you delay action by weeks, months, or years? Or will you choose to deal with it as soon as you recognize it? Thanks to my wife's question, I was able to flip the switch and ask myself what I was going to do about my IRS bill immediately. My first step was to call the IRS to understand my options.

I learned that to recover their money they would agree to set up a payment plan. I also learned I could negotiate the amount of my monthly payment. They originally stated I needed to pay $1,800 monthly for four and a half years. However, they eventually agreed to $700 per month, effectively reducing the amount I owed by two-thirds. I pulled up my bootstraps and I paid everything off. I made it my mission to pay off all my debts because I was determined not to go bankrupt.

You can call it a pride thing but I was determined to get myself out of the hole I dug without any outside help. I needed to feel that struggle to make sure I was never going to put myself in that situation ever again. I believe that luck happens when preparation meets opportunity. We have opportunities constantly; we just don't make use of them.

I became a formidable business owner because I'd learned how to run a successful business and I knew I never backed down from a challenge. When I had an opportunity to work at an RV dealership I took it and two years later, I bought the dealership. I grew the business from 20 employees to over 100 while growing revenue from $9 million to over $51 million a year in sales. By the time I sold the dealership to a publicly-traded company, I was completely debt-free.

However, all the things I learned and felt during that period didn't go away after that sale. I still have a hard time buying coffee or paying for lunch because of the thrifty financial habits I learned to practice.

## SET THE WORLD ON FIRE

When I was 29, I set goals, one of which was "FIRE." It's an acronym for Financially Independent, Retire Early. The concept is to have passive income that pays your bills so you can be financially free to do whatever else you want to do.

Most people think of retirement as sitting on a beach, but for me, retirement means the ability to follow your passion. I don't mean it like an Instagram meme that says follow your passion and you'll be happy. My passion led me to start the Money Talkers podcast because I want to help kids by giving them an opportunity that we don't normally do.

Kids don't get enough exposure to the world of financial literacy. While I can't change a century-old educational system, I can teach parents and their kids about finances. To me, the true benefit of having financial freedom is to have the resources to impact the world in my way. I want to offer what I have to kids so they can solve bigger problems and have real freedom in life.

I believe freedom is making decisions from a position of power and having the ability to make good decisions. Not to chase a dollar to spend it on something you bought a year ago. But to be able to go out there and find those passions and do the right things.

# MAKING THE WORLD BETTER, ONE PARENT AT A TIME

When I ask adults about where they learned about money, I always hear that it wasn't at home because their parents didn't talk to them about money. And it wasn't at school, either, because it's not part of the curriculum. This is a present and recurring problem that everyone agrees needs to be addressed.

I was very fortunate because I had entrepreneurial parents. My mom was very passionate about seeing me become successful. She was a stay-at-home housewife, but after we lost my dad she built her own company. I had an open relationship with her and we could talk about anything. She was a great friend and was always there for me to ask questions. We talked about things like sales, business, marketing, being an entrepreneur, and more. I've been talking about entrepreneurship since I was ten years old so of course, I started 13 companies!

I now understand my childhood and upbringing weren't typical. Most families don't have the conversations we did. No parent wants his or her kid to struggle because of money but most parents are uncomfortable discussing finances because many don't fully understand it themselves and it can trigger emotions. As parents, we don't want to look at ourselves in the mirror or get asked about the choices we have made in our lives. We often want our kids to come to us with questions when we feel they are "mature enough." But if you wait that long, they won't. Even though I talked about business with my mom, we never talked about money. Even when I was 24 years old with my own company, I still didn't know how to get car insurance.

It's easy to think that our kids will be okay because we "made it." But I've come to realize that's not how life works. You have to build that relationship along the way. You don't have to wait until the kids are mature before you start teaching them life and financial education. You need to be discussing with them the smaller things—financial information, bank accounts, and the like—at a young age.

There is not a lot of new stuff in the world of personal finance. There is a book entitled "The Richest Man in Babylon" that was written in 1926 by George S. Clason. It dispenses financial advice through a collection of fictional parables set 4,000 years ago in ancient Babylon. It's regarded as a classic of personal financial advice, and its lessons are still applicable today.

Currently, we are not providing answers for our kids even

though that's the work of the parents. There is nobody who loves us more than our parents. I would do anything for my kids, and I would die for them because I want the best for them. The hard question now is knowing what we can do about this frustration. My goal is so we can have a pathway and someone to say to our kids, "Hey, you know what, I'm going to go on this journey with you. I've done everything under the sun that you can think of. I've learned everything you can about finance, and I can guide you through it."

There are young adults at Wharton Business School who had to start a personal finance club because they didn't know anything about personal finance. Kids need this information but there is nobody to teach it except for the world. And that's a problem because the world is not geared to make money for you, but to make money off of you. If you make the decision to get into debt cycles, and you start leveling up by bringing in more money and debt, you'll also be bringing businesses more money, because that's what businesses are designed to do. At the end of the day, you will feel trapped.

It happens all too often but it doesn't have to continue. If we can start teaching kids about smaller important subjects, when those big decisions come down the road, we can be the ones they can trust enough to ask us questions.

This is the crazy journey I've been on. My Money Talkers podcast started from my desire to teach kids finance, but it has now evolved into a relationship-building exercise between parents and kids. The podcast is structured like a course. It starts by going through the basics and uncovers your "money story" at home. Then, we help you rewrite your money story.

I've always believed that the only thing we are given in life is a choice. If at any point, you are not happy about your money or finances or anything else, you have the choice to make changes. Finance is uncomfortable, but I aim to find people who can break the cycle and help their kids go change the world.

We can start by changing the discussion at the dinner table. Instead of asking your kids about their day or what they learned in school, you can start teaching them by talking about what possibilities are open to them.

By this, I don't mean just asking what they want to be when they grow up. I got asked that a million times as a kid, but back then I didn't even know what jobs were out there. My goal is to help parents start diving into relationships with their kids and help them mold their kid's critical thinking and financial skills. As a parent, you have to let them know there are millions of passionate jobs out there. Kids are eventually going to have these discussions but the idea is to start early having these conversations at home when the kids are younger. You can open their eyes to so many wonderful possibilities.

I open the doors for families to have a dialogue about money. I've realized that if more families start to have these conversations, we can change neighborhoods and trajectories. One of the things the wealthy do is that they talk about money. They have no fear of it, and they believe that money is a tool that you can control. They have an abundance mindset. I believe that if you start engaging in these conversations and start teaching financial stuff to your kids, it's then very difficult for them not to live what you are teaching. It's one of the things in Stephen Covey's "The 7 Habits of Highly Effective People." Learning to teach impacts more than just learning.

Talking about these things can also help to curb divorces because the majority of divorces happening in the United States and the world are due to financial hardships and differing financial views. If you teach your kids correctly and they are getting good information, you'll be offering them a better trajectory in life. That makes you a "Money Talker!" The impact of learning these vital pieces of information stretch beyond your home. I believe you will start making an impact in your community, too, because people will be drawn to you for financial information.

I have engaged a lot of people including random people, business owners, and high achievers. And what everyone agrees upon is that your mindset is more important than your actual work. This is why financial education is important.

## FINANCIAL KNOWLEDGE IS THE FASTEST WAY TO BUILD WEALTH

Think about this - according to data from the Census Bureau, Baltimore City Public Schools spent $16,184 per pupil, ranking among the highest spenders in the U.S. on a per-student basis. Yet the school system doesn't teach anything about entrepreneurship. To me, entrepreneurship is the fastest way to build wealth. Yes, entrepreneurship involves risk, but it's still the fastest way to build wealth and change communities.

Imagine that you are 16 years old and you put $10 a week into a Roth IRA returning nine percent. Or let's say you put that $10 into an S&P fund, or something with extremely low fees, like a Vanguard or Charles Schwab. If you consistently put $10 a week into an IRA, and you do nothing else for the rest of your life, by the time you are 76 years old, that $10 per week will return $2.1 million to you!

I've yet to meet a kid who wasn't mind blown by that illustration. I'll show them with a calculator how $38,000 multiplies to $2.1 million over the years. The reason kids are still surprised is because of how we think about people being winners. If you were to survey kids in high school and ask them if they could be a guaranteed millionaire, you would be pretty surprised at the answers. Kids would say stuff like, "I'm not good enough," or "I don't have the right connections," or "I came from the wrong neighborhood," and things like that.

This is a problem, because who's telling them that 80 percent of millionaires are self-made? Who's telling them that by saving $10 a week, you can be a millionaire when you retire? Yes, we tell them to get a good job and save money for retirement. But we're not using real numbers or real-life examples. We keep using these old cliches that I call Instagram memes. We should be instructing our kids to pay their bills on time and have good credit. If they ask why we should be telling them it's because it's going to cost them between $600,000 to $800,000 in interest over their lifetime to have bad credit.

Kids nowadays don't know that your credit determines the

interest rate you get. Let's say you want to buy a car. Fortunately, you have parents with good financial knowledge. Your parents understand credit and they advise you to save $2,500 by working for three months to build your credit. After you did this, they took you to a bank and they got you a secured credit card. That secured card will be able to get you a two percent interest rate on a $12,000 car. And, you can even decide not to get the car, and use the money for something else.

However, in another scenario with a different parent, the outcome is not so rosy. This time, your parents have no financial orientation. They simply told you to follow them to a car dealership and got you a car for $300 bucks a month. If this is what happens, you would be in the payment trap, because now you're paying 24 percent in interest instead of two percent. When you multiply that over a lifetime, you would lose $800,000 in investable dollars because you didn't care about credit.

When people say there's never enough money, I tell them it's because they weren't paying attention to their money leakages. Yes, you can have a car, but you don't have to pay a 24 percent interest rate. Currently, 78 percent of kids don't know what a credit score is, and there is a survey that found that 68 percent of Generation Z kids (born 1997 - 2015) want financial education. The good news is that kids are much more informed these days, and they know they need this stuff more than ever. They have been through the Great Recession, and now they are going through the COVID-19 Recession.

In the Money Talkers course, we are not just teaching what financial education is, we are teaching why you need it. We want you to see the numbers in front of you. We want kids to know that more wealth has been created in recessions than in bull markets. This way, they can get so far ahead in the game because they know all the advantages. Imagine if we could teach a million kids to be millionaires! That would be a trillion dollars produced!

I want you to know how much financial education benefits you. A lot of people want this education we teach at Money Talkers. However, most people spend years talking about what they want because they don't take action. This is the main difference between success and failure. Because success is not about where you're from or your education, it's about your personal decision to own it and go get it.

Here's an example. I asked for volunteers and 12 people went through their credit reports with me. I showed them the ins and outs of finances. I let them know that it's not scary if you can speak the language, and then we put an actionable plan in place. They were all able to increase their credit scores— some by over a hundred points. They all bought a home for the first time in their lives and opened retirement savings accounts after that. I was able to improve their determination by introducing them to concepts that changed the direction of their money story. They changed their family's trajectories by taking ownership.

That determination has been the driving source of my success for my entire life. I've always known that if there were other people out there who did it, you can do it too. So I always tell my kids that they don't fail and that they'll either learn or succeed. Yes, it may take you a long time to do things, but if you are determined, you can make the decision and do it.

## IMPORTANT FINANCIAL LESSONS TO NOTE

You should know that you can go get whatever you want. Don't let the world tell you anything different. You are always going to get a lot of advice but you have to choose your sources wisely. You want to emulate success as much as possible. To do this, you should be asking questions of those people who have the things you want. You want to know their mindset and how they think.

Unfortunately, most of us are not good with money and what I call "time wealth." But when you are young, you have something that most people don't realize. If you are respectful and you are trying to gain leadership in your life, you should know that mentors who are older than you are ready to help you. We want to help because we are not as time wealthy as you are but we see possibilities you don't see. This is how the world works. If you are a young person reading this, realize that if you ask successful people for advice, possibly by asking them to a lunch where you just pick their brains, you can learn a lot. You can get a lot out of talking to us about how we view money, entrepreneurship, and successful mindsets.

If you're constantly consuming mindless thoughts and media, your brain will seek validation from those things. If you want to be successful and financially free, able to travel the world and see all the possibilities life has to offer, you have to feed your brain with the right information. Your brain is like a muscle, and its condition will always reflect what you feed it.

If you want something in life, decide to change your inputs. Start following leaders and successful people. The simple mindset shift you will get from doing this is what makes the difference. When you change your mindset, you will eventually manifest the things you want.

## CALL TO ACTIONS FOR YOU

If you're a parent reading this and you want the best for your children, financial education has to be a priority. It has to be your "why." Yes, you may be uncomfortable at the thought of talking about money with your kids, but you have to know it'll be detrimental if you don't talk about it with them. Your why has to be bigger than your fears. If it isn't, you won't take any action. It's more important than your anxiety to take the steps needed to help them.

You have to take the first steps forward to help them be financially better, open their eyes to entrepreneurship, and have a successful mindset, and seek successful information. It's your responsibility to do this. I believe financial and life education is something we don't give confidently enough to our kids. We downplay a lot of things for them. We tell them that they can be anything they want to be. That's great, but how?

How do they figure these things out? That's why you have to be there to hold their hands and guide them through part of the journey together. Try your best to get the right information into their heads, because that's all that's required. I would suggest getting involved with what we are doing at Money Talkers because I'll provide the necessary tools and training. I provide the plan so you know what to talk about with your kids. We are going to deconstruct things. Then there's the mastery session where we take the things we learn at surface level, crank them up, and learn how to make use of the financial tools available to us.

You can't depend upon getting lucky in life. You must prepare before an opportunity comes knocking so that when that once-in-a-lifetime deal arrives, you have already repaired your credit and saved some money. Great opportunities move fast, so if you are not prepared, they'll go right by to the more prepared person.

You have no control over the world and these opportunities. You only have control over yourself, and that's what you need to be responsible for. So when you help prepare your kids for the future, then when opportunities come up, people will be amazed at how "lucky" your kids are.

If you're a kid reading this, my recommendation is to start with a book that changed my life: *Rich Dad, Poor Dad* by Robert

Kiyosaki. It's a simple read and it pulls the curtain back on a lot of things. It will begin to change the way you see how the world interacts with money. Don't wait for people to teach you things. Seek information and ask questions. Take initiative. It's your right to do these things. It's all about two words: take action.

Taking action goes a long way in determining whether or not you will be successful in life. It doesn't guarantee you will be successful, but action increases your chances tenfold. You find more and more opportunities by doing what it takes to prepare. And also, if you are a young person, remember that the seniors are there to help you. If you come to us respectfully, we will use our experience to help you every time!

Cody

# Evans Putman

---

## WHAT IF FAILURE IS NOT AN OPTION BUT A REQUIREMENT?

*Evans Putman, Founder, Infinite Impact Coaching & Consulting and Host of the Infinite Impact Radio Podcast*
*www.EvansPutman.com*

---

*"When you change the way you look at things, the things you look at change."*

Dr. Wayne Dyer

---

When my wife and I found out we were going to have a daughter, I was in the middle of launching a new software product and business.

I soon discovered that the person I was working with on this venture was not trustworthy. Money was unaccounted for, tasks not completed, contractors were not being paid and the mobile software product was nothing but a wireframe - a sketch on a handful of pieces of paper. In the end, all the money and time I invested was flushed away and I was left with nothing but a depleted bank account and an abundance of anger and disappointment. To top it off, against the backdrop of an economic downturn, my newly pregnant wife was laid off from her job in the mortgage industry.

I'd poured all my time and savings into that business venture and now we were also looking at the loss of health insurance and my wife's salary. With a baby on the way, however, burying my head in the sand was not an option. I decided, "Even though I have to start over at square one, I've got to put back on my entrepreneur hat, get back to work and make things happen." Fast forward three years; I now had a freelance business that gave me the freedom to work from home, choose my hours, and spend valuable time with my daughter. Entrepreneurship rewarded me with the opportunity I'd always desired once I found out I was going to be a father. I wanted to work with my wife as a team to care for and spend time with my daughter from the moment she entered this world. I knew these would be memories that I could never get back if I didn't have this opportunity.

After our daughter turned one, my wife went back to work.

It was great having two incomes at first. However, our life eventually got to a point where we were both working too much. My wife and I were exhausted all the time, and I realized it was affecting our relationship and our family's quality of life. Because of our vastly different work schedules and sharing parental duties, we weren't getting to see each other or spend time together. I wanted to do better. I knew she wanted to spend more time with our daughter and I wanted to be able to say, "Hey, you no longer have to work. Why don't you stay at home?"

And then, that day arrived. My business - the one I started after I got burned and lost our cash savings - was doing well enough that I was able to tell my wife that she could quit her job and come home. I have to say that being able to do that made me feel like a success as a father, husband, and entrepreneur. But that feeling didn't last long.

Once again, the unexpected was about to happen. Within 24 hours of my wife quitting her job and for a variety of weird circumstances, I lost all my clients except one. In one day, I went from making more money than I had ever made before to barely having enough to cover the utility bills.

But like before, I knew I couldn't be defeated by what

happened. And yes, it took me a day or two of feeling sorry for myself, but I resolved not to let this hold me down. I knew I had to take action and start from square one again. And to do that, I needed to switch my mindset and look at what happened as a gift. Now, it was time to unwrap that gift and see what was inside.

## GETTING BACK UP AFTER LIFE HITS YOU

When I look back, I realized that even though I was making a lot of money, I wasn't happy. I spent too many hours working. I resented my clients. I wasn't present with my family, and I was struggling with stress and anger. Now that the pain had my attention, I started looking at how I was working. I decided that if I was going to have the life I desired for my family, I had to move away from a transactional business and also stop selling my services to anyone and everyone. After that decision, I became a specialist who charged based on client results instead of selling my hours.

That 24-hour period from feeling like a success to hitting bottom was like the universe conspiring to knock me out of my comfort zone so I was forced to reevaluate and adjust the way I was doing business and living my life. That pause allowed me to realize that I must transform into a business owner and free myself from the trap of being a business operator. There is a big difference between the two - the biggest being freedom. Without this unexpected gift that came disguised as a setback, I wouldn't have started this journey that has brought me here now, as I write this, another three years later.

As I mentioned earlier, after feeling sorry for myself for a couple of days, I stepped up, took action and I trusted. I knew my next client was out there and it would be someone whose goals fit my skill set. This time, I wasn't going to just sell hours; I wanted to help my next client achieve a *result*. After I made that decision, it didn't take long before I received a message out of the blue. Reading it, I could see the potential client was looking for something both below my pay grade and skillset. Normally, I would just hit delete and move on to the next option. However, for a reason I can't explain, I felt compelled to respond to the message. We met and after some digging, I was able to see his *why* - the real result he was seeking - was much grander than the initial project description. And for me, not only did Pat become my first client on this new phase in my entrepreneurial journey, but his project also became my biggest success story!

Pat became a mentor and a friend with whom I'm still in

touch. I helped him achieve his mission, grow his business, and get his message to his audience. And, the most fulfilling part of this client journey for me was that I helped him make a real difference in the lives of the people he served.

That was how what could have been the worst situation was instead transformed into a gift and at the time became the best thing that could have happened to my business.

Let's step back and look at how that happened. As I began working with Pat, I learned what goals and outcomes he wanted. Together, we focused on achieving those desired results. It was my first experience moving from selling hours to selling results, and we were gaining momentum fast for his business.

One big result Pat desired was to grow his podcast and its audience. He loved speaking and interviewing guests - sharing his and their messages and success stories to inspire others into action. I soon realized, long before we met, he also desired to create the type of business that gave him the freedom to spend more time with his wife and his daughters. And even cooler, he had achieved that goal. It was an interesting coincidence because as I've shared, it was something I wanted as well. As it is often said, "When the student is ready, the teacher will appear."

But just as quickly as we gained momentum in some aspects of the business, we hit a wall in potentially the most important part of the business. There was a problem generating consistent revenue. Our customers told us we offered great products and services and we had a large traffic source - a dedicated podcast audience. Sales, however, didn't reflect either of these positive factors. I was dedicated to getting the results he desired but it got to a point that I started feeling desperate. To solve the problem, I decided to get better at my job; I signed up for a marketing conference in San Diego.

## FOLLOWING YOUR INNER VOICE

I planned everything for San Diego. I purchased plane tickets and paid for the hotel in advance. I was ready to go. But then I started seeing ads for a different conference in Orlando. It was also a marketing conference. Once again, I got that same inexplicable but intuitive feeling that I'd had when I first saw Pat's message about his project. I felt like something was calling me to go to Florida, not San Diego. Briefly, I thought maybe I could swing both but then I found out they were taking place on the same weekend.

I had a decision to make.

I listened to my intuition, got refunds for my conference tickets, flights, and room. Instead of flying to California, I was going to Florida to attend Funnel Hacking Live, a marketing conference put on by the company ClickFunnels which was founded by Russell Brunson. From the moment I arrived, I felt this high energy level. The crowd energy was more like a large sporting event than what I expected from a business conference. As I listened to the speakers, I got chills and goosebumps and felt as if there was an invisible tap on my shoulder and an inner voice saying, "Pay attention. This is for you." Something was telling me that this conference was my time to step up, shine, and play a bigger role in life and business.

After that conference, things were never again the same for me. It created an external shift in my business and an internal shift in myself. It was through that conference that I can say I made the first investment in myself. When I returned home, it was with a refreshed attitude and with coaches who were going to help guide me along the way. I didn't know if I had the solution for my client yet, but I had that feeling that things were going to change for the better. They did, indeed, and not just for my client; I also started seeing doors opening up for me. It was as if I had a new calling to take my business in a new direction.

When I look back on the series of events that got me to this point in my story, I see clearly that what felt like the worst moments - failures - were gifts hiding in plain sight. More importantly, I know with full conviction that my success and growth both personally and professionally wouldn't have happened if that rug hadn't been pulled out from underneath me on multiple occasions.

I wouldn't have had the opportunity to become resilient enough to take the next steps and take failure as a learning opportunity. With that in mind, one thing I now like to reflect on regularly and share with others is that failure is not an option; it is a requirement. We often think failure is something we should avoid but this isn't true. I believe that failure is a requirement for all types of growth—be it personal, business, or some other aspect of our lives. If it weren't for those failures of mine, I wouldn't be where I am today.

Instead of defaulting to returning to basically what amounts to employee status by trading hours for dollars, I was able to say "yes" to my intuition. I replied to that "out-of-the-blue" message. Even though it looked like a job below my skill level, it turned out to be the exact thing I needed to propel me forward on my journey. The point I want you to take away from this is that you never know when failure is going to happen. You just need to know that you have to go through it because there is an opportunity for transformation waiting on the other side.

## CREATING A POSITIVE RIPPLE EFFECT THROUGHOUT THE WORLD

One thing I believe deep down is that each of us has a mission and a message that will leave a positive impact on the world. I also believe there are people out there waiting to hear your truth - a message that will change their lives. My goal as a coach and consultant is to inspire and empower other entrepreneurs to rise into their authentic selves, to shine their truth into the world, and to create profitable and purpose-driven businesses.

I am creating a movement of what I like to call *Impact Influencers*. An Impact Influencer is anyone who creates positive ripples of impact by being, doing, and giving. An Impact Influencer has a mission that becomes a movement that transforms the lives of those they were meant to serve. This is my dream, my calling, and the seed that was planted during my experience in Orlando at my first Funnel Hacking Live.

I've been blessed to be invited on many podcasts, virtual

summits, high ticket coaching events, and other speaking oppor-tunities and often share this dream of starting a movement of Impact Influencers with the hosts and their audiences. During these discussions, one topic I like to talk about is the challenge we all feel when we start going after our dreams. We often have this feeling within us referred to as "imposter syndrome." We fall into the comparison trap and start feeling like we are not good enough.

I felt that, too. I didn't always feel like I'd "arrived." Back then, I was always feeling like I needed to be someone. What I like to say to people today is that you have a choice; when you start having those imposter feelings you can choose to put yourself in a place where you are constantly becoming who you want to be. You can keep telling yourself, "I'm becoming that person. I'm working on it. I'm learning and reading and doing my morning rituals." But the fact is that you will probably never accomplish your calling, achieve your dream, and make a positive contribution to those lives you want to change until you start *being*.

That's the key. You have to stop *becoming* and start *being*. Helping people make this transformation is one of my goals. My dream is to help people see their inner greatness. However, before I started this journey, I was that person who felt like he had to become something. It wasn't until I started making myself be that person that I started transforming my life. I had to stop thinking about becoming that future self I wanted for my family and my business. Instead, I chose to be that person right now.

I have a story I like to share with people to help them get over imposter syndrome. It came to me during meditation. I had a vision of myself and Tony Robbins standing on the roadbed of a metal truss bridge. It reminded me of the bridge I walked over many times as a young boy while visiting my grandparents in the mountains of North Carolina. In my vision, there was a section of the river directly under the bridge which was still as a lake before once again meeting the rocks where it began to move swiftly. As I glanced out of the corner of my eye at Tony Robbins, doubt-filled my mind and I thought, "There is absolutely no way I can create the kind of positive impact in the world that Tony creates. Should I just give up?"

I then noticed, in my peripheral vision, that Tony was leaning back slightly from the waist up holding something very large and heavy with both arms. I turned and faced him and saw it was a massive boulder. I then felt something in my left hand so I looked down and I was holding a small rock the size of a golf ball.

Seconds later, I noticed Tony step towards the bridge's railing and I watched as he leaned forward and dropped his boulder over the edge. When the boulder hit the water, it created a huge splash and big, forceful ripples that quickly traveled in a circular pattern out towards the shore.

As soon as the water calmed, an inner voice whispered to me urging me to drop my stone. Once again, I questioned why I should even bother because all I had was a small golf-ball sized rock to offer. The voice urged me once again to drop my stone. So leaned forward, straightened out my left arm, opened my hand, and let go.

I dropped my small stone over the edge, and guess what happened when it hit the water? Even though the impact was not as strong or as forceful as Tony's, it also created a circle of ripples that traveled just as far and did not stop until they reached the shore.

The ripples in my vision represented the positive effect you can have on the world when you put your message and mission out there. The takeaway is that it doesn't matter where you are on your journey. It doesn't matter if you feel like you are not as good as the people you perceive as more successful than you. Stop comparing yourself to others and just take action and let go of expectations.

If you change just one life with your message, that one life can change the lives of ten other people, and those ten can then change the lives of a hundred people, and so on. It doesn't matter where you are now. As long as you decide to be and to put your message out there, you will change the world.

## TWO KEY LESSONS LEARNED ON THE JOURNEY

Throughout my journey over the past years, I've learned two key lessons. The first important lesson is to surround yourself with a network of friends, mentors, and coaches who can help you grow and to whom you can speak openly. These people will encourage you to keep chasing your mission and your dreams when other people in your life don't understand what you are going through as an entrepreneur.

Life becomes especially intricate when you are both a parent and an entrepreneur. You'll try to fulfill multiple roles, and as those of us in this pursuit know, entrepreneurship can be quite lonely. Without surrounding yourself with a strong network of like-minded entrepreneurs, coaches, and mentors, you can quickly find yourself isolated and giving in to your fears and doubts.

I mentioned earlier that it was not until I decided to invest in myself that my life and my business changed for the better. I invested in a coaching program and along with my coach I also connected with other like-minded entrepreneurs. Since taking that first step and as I've grown to new levels in my business, I've invested more and more in myself. I went on and found other coaches who could help me get over the other bumpy areas of my life.

Before we get to the second lesson, I want to offer some important advice for hiring a coach. If the coach you are considering doesn't have a coach, find someone else. It is crucial that the person you invest in also invests in themselves, and leads by example.

I've probably used this coaching analogy a million times. I find myself coming back to it again and again because basketball was always an escape for my younger self. I was also blessed with the opportunity to share my love for the sport as a coach for young children at the Boys and Girls Club as well as coaching a high school team with players who have gone on to play in college and the NBA. Coaching is vital, and it's a thing common to all high-performing people. Michael Jordan is arguably the best basketball player to ever play the game. He didn't rise into his greatness alone; he had coaches. He didn't just have coaches who were coaching his teams; he also hired personal trainers to get his fitness level up to where it needed to be to perform at a high level. The fact is that the best of the best are always investing in coaching. If you want to be your best personally and professionally, you should invest in coaches too.

## TIME IS WEALTH

I learned this second important lesson directly from my former coach Myron Golden, a very successful entrepreneur, who regularly shared that wealth is measured more in time than money. As Myron says, "Money can be replenished, but time cannot."

As someone who got into entrepreneurship intending to create a lifestyle that puts family first, time freedom has always been my priority. Earlier in my career, I didn't understand how to get that freedom and it caused a lot of issues. As mentioned previously, trading time for money created a situation where I was forced to work long hours to keep money flowing in my business. I became resentful towards my clients because I felt they were responsible for taking away my time freedom. And even when I wasn't working, the stress it put on me kept me from being fully present with my wife and daughter.

Working with my coaching and consulting clients and talking to other entrepreneurs, I realize that most are still struggling to get that freedom. Yes, we want monetary freedom. But when you boil it down, we all want to figure how to create more "time freedom" to do what we want to do - spend more time with family and friends, take a vacation, or travel. Wealth will always be measured more in time than in money.

The problem I see many of my coaching and consulting clients experience is that in the process of looking for that freedom by starting their own business, they end up creating a job for themselves. They end up working more hours than most people in the corporate world, and they get paid less. Unfortunately, it is often a symptom of entrepreneurship. Who in their right mind would give up a job with security and a good paycheck to work twice as hard and get less money? It's mind-boggling, but there's a solution to that—and I learned it the hard way.

I have come to realize that if you want that time freedom, you have to do specific things. The biggest differentiator is to be a business *owner* and not a business *operator*. I was a business operator for most of my career. If I didn't work, the money didn't come in, and that placed a constraint on my time freedom. I was selling one-to-one services and was always the final decision maker in my business. Even though I hired others and we worked together as a team, I was the hub of the wheel. Nothing operated when I was not around. And yes, that was 100% my fault.

Working with my coaches and through real-world experience with clients, I discovered that I had to move from the business-operator zone into the business-owner zone. To create time freedom, you must move from selling one-to-one to selling one to many. You must find a core premium service which provides massive value to all your clients and focus on giving them one big result.

You must also find ways to reduce work created by the ways you market and sell your products and services. Experience taught me that the model of multiple offers with frequent launches won't provide you with the freedom you desire. The secret is to find a core product or service that you can sell at a high ticket premium price to your clients. This product or service must give your clients massive value and a big, transformational result while also freeing you from the constant work of fulfilling day in and day out. This is the type of business that you want.

The main theme is to *simplify* your products and service. Have one simplified service or product that creates the transformation your clients want. When you create that transformation for your clients, you create dream clients for life. These clients are more enjoyable and fulfilling to work with and they become your biggest fans and refer business to you regularly.

If you want to learn more about attracting and serving high ticket dream clients, go to www.EvansPutman.com. You'll find my free, private podcast Message to Millions which delivers coaching directly to your smartphone and favorite podcast player. You'll learn the exact processes I've used to increase income, ignite impact, and transform lives while also achieving the time freedom we all desire by creating a profitable, scalable dream client business.

# FINDING THAT ONE THING THAT CHANGED EVERYTHING

When I reflect on my entrepreneurial journey, I always fondly remember the lessons learned while helping my client Pat. I helped him quickly grow his struggling podcast to over 150,000 monthly listeners which felt like a big win. However, at the same time, I hit a brick wall because I couldn't generate consistent revenue for the business.

This was unacceptable because I was the marketing and sales consultant he hired to solve this very problem and I now found myself struggling to deliver on that promise. I applied different tactics and strategies which were proven to be successful with other clients, but with Pat's business, I felt like I was pushing a boulder uphill. Just when I felt like we were getting momentum, something would cause us to slip, lose traction, and roll backward. Then, I'd have to start pushing all over. We just couldn't get to the point where the boulder was rolling effortlessly downhill.

I got into that desperation mode I talked about earlier. I did things I know now were mistakes including defaulting to repetitive launches and commodity-pricing promotions. I decided

I had to find a solution or I wasn't going to have the client anymore. And it wasn't losing the client that was my major concern; it was the fact that I enjoyed working with him. I wanted to see him succeed because he was an entrepreneur with a message and a mission. He wanted to create a positive impact and change lives. He was an entrepreneurial dad who had unlocked the secret of how he could be highly successful with his business while creating the freedom to spend quality time with his wife and daughters. Now, he wanted to share how other entrepreneurs could do the same.

I felt that connection with him because of my daughter. I saw him as a mentor and not just a client. I was desperate, and that was why I went to the ClickFunnels event. At first, I thought that I was going to learn some magic tactics and little-known secret strategies and shortcuts that were just going to flip the switch and make things better.

Right as the first speaker, Russell Brunson, took the stage, I discovered success did not come as a byproduct of tactics, hacks, secrets, and shortcuts.

I learned that as an entrepreneur you spark the fire of success when you first *connect with your message*. Next, I discovered that unlike the spider web of confusion that we had created before in our business, there was a simple thread that ran through everything. And not only did this discovery change the business, it changed my life as well.

My client's business changed so much that within twelve months, I saw it go from revenue of basically zero dollars to $500,000 without relying on paid advertising. We achieved this level of success by removing complexity in our business and simplifying the company's message into one core idea, one core target audience, one core offer, and one core delivery and fulfillment method.

We simplified the business down to a premium offer and service that would create a big desired transformation for one person - our ideal listener-customer. When we did that we achieved momentum. That's how we got the boulder over the peak and rolling downhill. In one of the testimonial case study videos I filmed with Pat, he said it even got to the place where his business became a virtual ATM.

It was so simple and effortless that all he had to do was get on the podcast and just do what he loved and the money started pouring in. We no longer had to rely on tactics because we were creating transformation in people's lives. We were relying on sound principles that produced results.

Once he achieved those results, I put systems in place so he could continue running his business, and my work for him was done. After I left, his business continued to grow into a sellable, seven-figure business. It became marketable and desirable to others because of multiple factors including the simple structured system that practically ran on auto-pilot. There was also the highly-engaged audience of 4.5 million-plus podcast listeners along with the email list comprised of high-value leads and customers.

In the end, because we built his business the right way, my client was eventually able to sell his podcast and company for a nice sum of money and go do something else he wanted to do. And that's the story of how we went from running a struggling podcast to changing people's lives and having a seven-figure business.

On the flip side, this situation isn't just about how his failing business turned into a success, it's also about how it changed my life personally and professionally. Because as I sat there in that ClickFunnels event listening to the speakers share stories of changing lives, I chose to take action. I decided to invest in myself with coaching, altering the direction of my business.

I realized I was being called to serve others and to help

create an impact. I focused on making myself a better person, a better father, a better husband, and a better entrepreneur. I hired a coach to help me, and I was able to change my family's life. Not only that, I was able to impact many more lives through my business. At one point, I had a breakthrough idea in my morning meditation. Four words came to me, and those four words now form the core foundation I base my business around: *Rise, Shine, Simplify, and Serve.*

Those four words are the framework of the *Infinite Impact Method™ - An Entrepreneur's Path to Prosperity and Purpose.* With this new framework, I feel like I'm finally fulfilling my mission and contributing to creating a larger impact on the world. It helps me be rather than waiting to *become.* Since then, I've been helping other entrepreneurs fulfill their mission and purpose. Among other things, I help them monetize their message and create a movement that generates positive impact ripples that change the world.

The foundation of my business came from the seed of failure and it grew into what it is today by trusting and following my intuition. That inner voice guided my decision to step out of my comfort zone, take a leap of faith, and to invest in myself which brought me to where I am today.

Today, I serve others without being concerned about winning awards for myself. I was asked recently on a podcast if my goal was to win the Two Comma award from ClickFunnels which celebrates earning one million dollars with your business. I replied, "No, my goal is to help a hundred other people win their awards over the next year. I know that by helping others achieve their awards, I'll get the true reward of knowing that I'm changing the world for my daughter."

## ENTREPRENEUR FIRST, FATHER ALWAYS

Before I ever thought about becoming a father, I chose to be an entrepreneur because I wanted total control over my life. I wanted to be independent and I didn't want to work for somebody else and be tied to their schedule. My decision was a selfish one. But after I became a father, entrepreneurship took me on a journey of self-discovery and helped me become a better person so I could put in the effort to give my best each day to my daughter.

From the moment I became a father I felt driven to become the best father possible for my daughter because I had a difficult experience with my father. I knew my goal but I didn't yet know how to achieve it. Like most of us, I saw myself as a work in progress.

In the last two decades I've launched and sold multiple businesses but it wasn't until my daughter was born that my entrepreneurship focus changed. I decided to become a better person, and my daughter helped bring out the best in me. She has also inspired me to focus my business on helping others create a positive impact and change the world. If it weren't for fatherhood and entrepreneurship, I would not be the person I am today, and I would not be living the life I am living today to serve others.

It's been amazing to watch my daughter grow into a beautiful, kind, compassionate, and loving person. I'd like to pat myself on the back for all her wonderful qualities but I must first tip my hat to her amazing mother who embodies the same special qualities. Working from home, I get the added benefit of seeing my daughter's creativity shine each day. I've watched proudly as she taught herself how to start her own YouTube channels. She crafts stories, creates animated characters, adds soundtracks and sound effects, and pulls it all together in her videos. It's such an amazing gift to witness her use her creativity. I know she's meant for great things, and no matter what, she's going to have the resilience to follow her dreams and make her path one which changes lives for the better. I'm so proud of her and blessed and grateful to be her father.

Those are my major rewards and lessons learned so far on my journey. I'll also take this opportunity to thank the other authors and parents in this book. You probably read some of their stories before mine. I believe they are all amazing human beings, and they each focus on serving others to make the world a better place for our children and future generations. I would advise you to take advantage of everything that you are offered in this book.

Lastly, I would like to leave with you the four core words that eventually formed the foundation of my Infinite Impact Method™ coaching program. Those four words are Rise, Shine, Simplify, and Serve. It doesn't matter if you are a dad or mom or a young person reading this; I would advise you each day to rise into your authentic self, shine to affect others positively, simplify to take quantum leaps in your life, and serve selflessly to transform lives. And remember these three things: listen to your inner voice, follow your calling, and launch your dream business. The world needs your gifts!

If you need help getting started or taking the next big step, come to EvansPutman.com and get free access to my Message to Millions private podcast which offers free coaching directly to your smartphone and favorite podcast player app. I update the private podcast regularly with everything I'm learning and using to help my clients monetize their message and build profitable, dream client businesses that change lives. I also encourage you to download my public podcast Infinite Impact Radio from Apple Podcasts and listen to the inspiring stories of entrepreneurs - Impact Influencers - who I am lucky enough to interview. And once you launch your dream business and you start changing the world, reach out to me and let's share your story on Infinite Impact Radio too!

Thank you!

Evans

# Akbar Sheikh

## IS FAILURE THE KEY TO YOUR SUCCESS?

*Akbar Sheikh, CEO at www.AkbarSheikh.com, Philanthropist, Best-Selling Author*

> *"If you are looking forward to retirement, something is wrong."*
> Akbar Sheikh

I come from a family of entrepreneurs, several generations deep. As a matter of fact, at a recent family gathering, everyone present was an entrepreneur except for a doctor and a lawyer. My dad has eight brothers and seven sisters and they are all in business.

So, my family is kind of interesting. Now, I'm not one of those who thinks entrepreneurs are better than other people. I only think it's important to say I wasn't brainwashed like most people. My siblings and I did not grow up in a household that had a scarcity mindset, nor were we conditioned to seek a cubicle-based career.

We never talked about money and our family business had its ups and downs, but we were groomed to be entrepreneurs. While I was growing up, my dad's business struggled. I mention this because my dad never taught his kids financial literacy, probably because he wasn't financially literate himself. His dad died when he was still very young and there weren't many people around to teach him about investment and diversified income so he was not fiscally well-rounded and he certainly wasn't the greatest finance manager. He started his business at a young age and ran it, together with his brothers. There were times he was making an unbelievable amount of money but he kept reinvesting all of it into that one business without diversifying his sources of income. This is the reason he struggled.

When I was still living at home, I anticipated that I would probably take over my dad's retail business eventually. When I was a kid, I can remember that I often had fun in the store playing with my siblings. I didn't want to stay home and watch Saturday cartoons. Although my dad worked all day and I just walked around the store like an idiot sometimes, my siblings and I still had fun and it was interesting.

But problems started right after I got out of college. I became lost and confused because I realized that I completely hated retailing. I hated it because I considered it to be a man-made prison. We had furniture stores, merchandise stores, and things like that. But I just wasn't a retailer. Back then, I often had the idea of opening a mattress store. I graduated with a degree in business and yet the moment I returned to the store, I was overcome by just how much I completely hated retailing!

When I got a little older I started selling cars. A cousin of ours came around and taught us about auctions. I remember buying cars at auction for around $800 bucks and then selling them for more. Selling cars shifted me into hustling mode. I enjoyed it a lot and it ended quite well. **This is why I always say that you have to understand your strengths and weaknesses.**

Not to brag, but I think I'm a good salesman. When it comes to selling, I can sell you paint off the wall. Selling is just natural for me. Nobody sold cars the way I did. However, all the money I made eventually disappeared. I lost everything because I was financially illiterate. Nobody thought to teach me accounting or how to diversify and invest so I ended up wasting a lot of my income and for many years I was broke. Now I know financial literacy is really important - even more so than selling.

I think selling is easy. You might be good at the financial literacy thing while thinking you don't know how to sell anything. **My message for you is to concentrate on your strengths and recruit around your weaknesses.** If you suck at sales, then get your own sales team.

Back in the day, I did my own sales calls. Now when I think about it, I see that it was probably a waste of my time because I was able to build a sales team and they were closing right around 30%. I still took sales calls every day when I didn't have to because my team was performing well. Now I wonder what would have happened if I had spent that time learning finance rather than doing what I already knew how to do. If you don't know how to sell, get a team. If you don't understand finances, find someone to teach you the processes and systems. You'll be better off by doing so. **Don't ignore your financial education because it is important.**

Back then, I was just lost. I didn't want a job because it wasn't programmed in me. I didn't understand the concept of having, or listening to, a boss who yells at you and then gives you a little bit of money at the end of the month. So I didn't want a job, but at the same time, I hated retail. I believed I wasn't a good businessman. So, I was in that confused state in my life where I didn't know what to do.

## MAKING A DECISION NO ONE WILL MAKE FOR YOU

This confusion about what to do with my life led me down a dark path. I ended up with a very unhealthy lifestyle: I put on too much weight, I developed a crippling anxiety disorder, I mingled with bad company regularly, and I ended up getting married to the devil. I wasn't spiritual and my life became a total mess. I eventually hit rock bottom when I landed in the hospital half-dead from partying too much.

But, God saved me and I took advantage of that turning point in my life. I made a decision no one was able to make for me. I decided to change the direction of my life. I went completely organic and stopped eating junk food. I paid attention to my health and started practicing yoga. I began to drink a lot of water every day and lost about 60 pounds. I started praying and became more spiritual. I got rid of all my toxic friends; they were shocked because I was close to them but I simply disconnected without any explanation. I changed my personality from being the rockstar party animal to being a respectable human being.

Before that turning point, people in my extended family kept their kids away from me because I was a bad influence. Today, those same people send their kids to me for summer internships. And that is a point I'm illustrating for you: **the truth is that you can be anyone you want to be.** You just have to make some changes. They may not be the world's easiest changes but if you want to, you can... because that's exactly what I did.

I worked hard on myself. And as I was doing this, I temporarily lived with my brother in a closet. It was pretty wild because there were no windows, and I didn't even have access to a shower or hot water. But, it was fun despite that because I had started on a better path. I looked on Craigslist for something to do and that was how I discovered internet marketing. I remember feeling that I had found my big guarantee. Immediately, I felt like Neo in the Matrix because I could understand the psychology behind everything I was seeing. I knew why the ladies in the adverts were always smiling, and I knew why online websites use big red buttons!

I knew I had to get involved; cutting a long story short, I sold my car for $2,000, I signed up with a network marketing company, I hired a coach, and *here I am years later as one of the top 1% global earners because I made a decision to change my life and I paid attention to my strengths!*

## KEY MISSION STATEMENTS

My business's major mission statement is very clear — our mission is to Make More and Give More. We have been growing every single month and trying our best to achieve this. With every action taken, we are always asking the question, "Is this going to help people to make more so they can give more?"

I have an industry-leading coaching program. It helps people wrap a thriving business around their unique information and talent. We help people build thriving businesses and we ask the vital questions: what do they need and how do they start - and then we help them find the way.

The coaching business is 90% mental, so the first module of our program helps to rewrite the mind, body, and soul. We believe this is the first step in the preparation for massive success. The remaining modules teach how to create incredible offers and more. You learn how to build funnels that convert to sales, and we give out templates that you can start using right away. After that, you are shown how to market everything for free, and how to sell more, scale, and grow your business.

I plan to help people achieve great success. We support people daily and we help them achieve breakthroughs. But there's one problem we struggle with and that's the fact that more than 90% of people never finish a course. Most people just watch the first module and even then, they don't implement what they learn.

Because we are determined to solve this problem we have hired someone to make CliffsNotes of our course. So, as people go through the program, they'll be able to see the action items as bullet points. We are moving towards an institutional arena where teaching others becomes more hands-on. Imagine building a coaching business over the weekend. That's the direction my business is moving towards.

Our number one mission is to make our coaching program a more instructional, concise, and fill-in-the-gap style. Because our ultimate goal is for more people to be successful so they can make more to give more, we are making it as simple as possible for people to consume our material and implement it.

Our number two mission is to do more live events and

workshops, virtual and in-person. These workshops will run for a few days, be action-packed, and energetic. We'll walk our students through the entire process of creating awesome offers and help them build high-converting funnels that we send traffic to right away.

Our number three mission is to build a community around the business. We continue to grow our brand around our vision to "Make more, Give more." We foster an atmosphere where every one of our partners feels like they are part of a community. We dive more into lifestyle changes because that was the first step I took on my journey to such massive success.

## BEING CAREFUL OF EXTERNAL INFLUENCES

To be honest, I believe my lifestyle played a huge part in my 'decade of destruction' as I refer to it. Back then, I couldn't succeed in business no matter how hard I tried. I became mentally and physically unhealthy because my environment was unhealthy. I look clean and lean now, but back then, I looked like a cheeseburger. Now that I know more, I understand the reason why I now succeed.

There is a saying that you are what you eat. This is very true. And while it's true that you can't judge a book by a cover, I say there are exceptions to everything. If you saw me ten years ago, I looked like a big fat slob and that was exactly what I was. My bank account, car, business finances, relationships, and everything combined created a toxic disaster.

I have integrated lifestyle changes into our community because my goal is to help people organize and improve every aspect of their life and I am an example that all these things are connected. Going forward we may offer supplements, customized diaries, and more to help our community succeed faster. I draw and write in my diary every day and I think it's helpful.

The fact is that your lifestyle and the things you surround yourself with matter. If your partner, friends, clients, and team are people from hell, then your life will be hell. It's that simple. If the people in your life are heavenly people, then your life will be heavenly. I've been on both sides of the spectrum so I have firsthand experience. **My goal is to help people to get unbelievable teams, relationships, and partners.** I want them to live a remarkable lifestyle. I don't just want them to feel better, I want them to be physically, mentally, spiritually, and financially healthier.

## THINKING LIKE A WINNER

We have helped a lot of people achieve six-, seven-, and eight-figure incomes. But you know what? At the end of the day, our dream clients are not the newbies who have never had any success in their lives. Nor are they the ones looking for a lottery ticket and an easy win. They are the winners. Now, I'm not here to label people but I've realized that at the end of the day, **winners always win.**

One of the first things I learned in my industry is that the difference - between those who make it and those who don't - is **the scope of their action and speed of their implementation.** The people I end up helping the most are the people with hunger and passion for success. These are the people to whom we end up giving trophies. And that's the thing about successful people; you can't teach this drive. Sometimes it lies dormant as it did with me for a decade. Sometimes it never surfaces; my brother lives in a house full of successful entrepreneurs and he doesn't have the hunger to succeed.

We help winners win more rapidly and easily through the use of our support and systems. We have helped a lot of people with just one shift; that's how simple it is. We give them suggestions such as changing how they think about their clients, how to tweak their traffic and sales strategy, and so on. This is where winners set themselves apart; the winners take hold of these suggestions and make something with them.

My mission is to work with entrepreneurs who have that drive in their hearts to assist them to make more so they can give more. I aspire to work with larger companies and help them scale their business growth rapidly and effectively. As I do this, I also want to live a well-balanced life. I would love to give time to my business, family, religion, and communities. I want a win-win situation for everyone. My vision is one of happiness, health, wealth, and spreading love. Lastly, I'm interested in leaving a legacy and that's why I'm involved in philanthropy; my wife and I run a non-profit helping communities access clean and safe drinking water.

## KEY LIFE LESSONS TO NOTE

Throughout my career, I've learned a lot about what benefits business. Success is not what you think. A lot of people believe that being successful online is about having some magical funnel, code, or some email sequence. The reality is quite different because success requires none of this stuff.

Our training explains everything about earning six figures monthly. I broke everything down into a step-by-step process and all my tactics for success are in the program. I want it to be completely transparent so everyone can see exactly what I do to make money. But success is not about magical or tactical stuff. If you ask me what marketing is I'll tell you it's about testing, tweaking, and scaling. What does that mean?

Let me explain with an analogy. Most online people are always sending out messages and offers. Let's imagine that you are one of these people. Your main problem is that your offer is not working. If this is the case, then all you need to do is to look at those people whose offers are working and model them. It's that simple. Tweak their process, and use that data to make your own more interesting.

I have a cool show called *"Eight Figure Coffee."* In each episode, I interview eight-figure earners ($10Million and above.) As I listen to people in these interviews, I'm exposed to - and learn - their secrets. Now, you are about to learn the same secrets.

In one episode one of my clients, Brian Page, shared one of his success secrets with me; he modeled other successful people. Being successful is not about magic. It's about being hungry and passionate, having drive and tenacity to take action and keep tweaking while modeling other successful people.

Take my weightloss story. I lost close to 60 pounds and there is no magic about what I did. If you are a fat person, it's all about eating a cleaner diet and exercising a little bit. I didn't have to do more than that to lose weight. Being a little more active is all you need. Eating a cleaner diet means eating good, wholesome food without corn syrup and sugar. The truth is that losing weight is very simple and the only problem is that no one sticks to simple plans.

People keep looking for a magical process where there is none. This is the reason the weight loss industry is a multi-billion dollar industry with endless pills that don't work. **The real secret to success anywhere is tenacity and hunger.** The reason I made it in everything I do is simply that I told myself that I was either going to make it work or die trying.

The lack of drive is a major problem with the people in internet marketing. There are a lot of non-entrepreneurs trying to be entrepreneurs. Many people rush to rash decisions and quit too early. I see people cutting the price of their products in half just because they are not having sales. Or someone may say that they tried doing webinars but they didn't work. In reality, they don't have enough data to jump to conclusions.

The internet is a platform for entrepreneurs to be entrepreneurs. The rules of success on the internet aren't different from those of real life. If only people knew how many times I've had to rewrite a script or video offer before it worked, people wouldn't be so quick to give up or change course.

**Nothing good comes easily.** I remember once I tried to get leads to one of my offers but my strategy wasn't working. I had to step back, delete the post, restructure it, and then try again several times before I got it right. This is what being an entrepreneur is all about. **An entrepreneur is tenacious and doesn't give up.**

Entrepreneurship is about being a problem solver, not an excuse-maker. While growing up, my dad once told me that an entrepreneur is a bulldozer. I agree with him. As an entrepreneur, you can't give up each time you face a problem. You need the mindset that you can achieve anything you want. And yes, you are going to face a huge amount of problems, but you don't have to let them stop you.

As for me, I'm a funny-looking man who is technologically illiterate. But, somehow I'm a top 1% internet marketer. That's a message for you. **You can be anything you want - if you want it enough.** Many people say that I'm a lucky guy. However, I believe there is no such thing as luck. Success is nothing but the choices we chose to make every single day.

## A LESSON IN PAYING ATTENTION

That said, the other success secret I've learned is focused work. It is obvious, isn't it? If I'm going to test, tweak, and scale, I'm going to need to put a message out there. If it doesn't work, I'm going to need to do it again and again. There is no way I can do this without eliminating all distractions. I have to be able to concentrate on what I'm doing.

This is easier said than done these days. What I see everywhere I look are endless distractions. There are constant emails, Facebook notifications, Snapchat, Instagram, Youtube, Voxer, TikTok, and so on fighting for our attention. The truth is that these social media platforms are designed for one purpose — to get you hooked and keep you addicted.

They are like drug dealers and their job is to make you keep coming back for another hit. They want you hooked so they can sell more ads and make more money. And they are succeeding on a massive scale. Most people are addicted to these platforms, and it's getting to a point that they are not getting anything done because brilliant minds were hired by the various platforms to design their algorithms to be addictive.

And this is where it gets interesting because it's entirely different for successful people. They are not glued to these platforms and they turn off their notifications. I've done the same; I won't know if anyone calls me unless I intentionally check my phone. It's then that I can decide to call them back or not. If aliens looked down on us from above, they would conclude that we are very sick. It's just sad because being distracted will get you nowhere. **The killer combination for succeeding is focused work mixed with tenacity.** That's how to easily get to the top.

Another success secret that I've learned is to put your customer first. A lot of people are not customer-focused. They just want to sell and sell, and they are not even worried about the quality of their product. You can only lose by thinking about yourself and your success alone. Experience has taught me that you can never lose by putting your client first. **You can never lose by giving.**

Lastly, don't take too much on yourself. Try to do what you do best and outsource the rest. Take it easy, be moderate in your business, have the right intentions, pay attention to your health, and spend valuable time with your family.

## TURNING YOUR PAIN INTO PROFIT

Failure is your best friend. As an entrepreneur, you shouldn't see failure as the end. Entrepreneurs should not think in that context. If I have my way, I would make a motion to replace failure with words such as opportunity, gold, accelerator, and so on.

In my business, we make 99% of our money organically and in fact, my clients and I have made multiple seven-figures organically. But, recently I put up an offer that flopped. Within 45 minutes, I deleted it and put up another one and it flopped again. Again, I took the data, tweaked the copy to make the post more casual, and then more formal, and still, nothing happened. Next, I told myself to do a mixture of what I had done earlier. I made it more colorful and guess what? It failed yet again. It took me a long time before I finally got the messaging copy targeted correctly. I did varieties of offers: long, short, casual, serious, entertaining, etc. It still didn't take off. However, the lesson in this is that I eventually got it right.

The problem I see all the time out there is that people rush to make decisions. They try to reduce price and they quit too early. I tell these people that they don't have enough failure data to make those decisions. Did they talk to at least a hundred people before making their decisions? Did they try a hundred times before quitting?

If you have seen my photo where I'm wearing a blue blazer having received my first Two Comma Club Award for generating $1Million in revenue, you will see me with a perfectly black beard without a single white hair. But if you look at me now, most of my hair is white. The thing is that these gray hairs are very expensive. It's like playing a video game; I have spent years collecting coins and experience.

All my gray hairs come from my failures, most business-related, and some personal. I can't remember the exact amount of time I paid six-figures to different traffic agencies for ads on Facebook, Instagram, and Youtube; all the money went down the drain. We have tried this strategy working with the small agencies, the big agencies, and the big retainers. Now, I'm not saying that there are no good traffic agencies out there; I can recommend a few. The lesson is I earned these gray hairs through my experience working with them so I now know how to deal with them more effectively.

Some of my clients ask me, "Hey, which is a good one?" I can give them a valuable answer because I've gone through failures that cost me so much money that I can spare my clients this pain. In essence, when you work with someone with experience who has the gray hairs to prove it, what you are paying for is perspective. This is the reason I can come into your business and offer valuable advice quickly. It's because I've been there and I've done everything you can imagine.

These days I can see right away where people get it wrong. There is a broken model that a lot of people still use: the 90/10 rule. Many marketers spend 90% of their time marketing and 10% fulfilling their customer wishes. They keep going south and they have no fulfillment process.

In my business, we are completely different. We are dedicated to helping people and we encourage them to achieve great success. So, we are always getting success stories every single week. If you are involved in the 90/10 marketing model, I want to encourage you not to do it any longer. We know it doesn't work and that is why we are heavily invested in our backend for the fulfillment of our promises.

We even have someone we pay very well to act as the Director of Client Success. We invest heavily in our backend because we are customer-focused. As I always say, **you'll never go wrong being client-success focused.** You can never go wrong by giving. But, I didn't just learn this in one day. It's the realization born from years of experience.

## MAKING USE OF THE GOOD OLD GRAY HAIRS

For two years my wife has been working on her companies. Recently, she did a photoshoot for her product. This is something I have experience with. When we did my first professional photo shoot for my first product, we went to one of those discount stores and bought props. We set up the props, got a photographer from Craigslist for $500 bucks, did the photoshoot, and returned the props afterward.

However, my wife didn't consult me before she did her recent photoshoot. The photographer then messed her up by telling her that she could only get a certain amount of images. When I looked into it, I realized she needed more pictures but the photographer insisted that we didn't make a deal for more. And that's the trick. If she had consulted me, we would have made a deal with the photographer saying we own all the images. That's a failure on her part; she has learned her lesson. The truth is that failure is in every part of the business and if you are listening, it will always teach you something.

One common question people ask me is how do I handle

a customer or client who doesn't play with the group and is dedicated to sabotaging themselves. Most times, those asking these questions are ready to call out these people. But I don't think that's wise. My advice is to be nice. Talk to them and see what's going on with them. This is some of what I've uncovered from experience and my many failures.

It's remarkable how much you need failure to succeed. You have to go through several funnels and numerous phone calls to get the one that works. You have to turn your pain into profits. To succeed as an entrepreneur, you need to have thick skin.

Years back, a guy left my mastermind program because he believed he was not getting enough support from me. Hearing him say that was like a punch to my gut. I felt hurt but the painful lesson taught me to double my effort. By doubling my support for clients, my success stories went up and people stayed on board for longer, meaning I significantly improved customer retention.

I had happier clients because I was able to turn my pain into profit. So, an entrepreneur needs thick skin. I won't say you should go drive an Uber if you don't have thick skin. You just have to work on getting it. Be prepared to get punched in the gut regularly.

In my coaching business, we get clients' success stories every single week. As long as you have the right coach, the right plan, and you don't give up, you will eventually succeed. The truth is that you haven't truly failed unless you give up - all other failures are simply teachable moments. You just have to stay focused and tenacious. Failure is your friend. Without failure, there can be no success. So my advice is to keep failing and enjoy yourself while you do. Enjoy it because each time you fail, it takes you one step closer to success. There is a family story that sums this up perfectly.

Sara Blakely, the founder of the billion-dollar hosiery and apparel company Spanx, relayed this story at a Network for Teaching Entrepreneurship event in New York City. She recounted that every night at the dinner table, her father, an attorney, would ask her and her brother what they had failed at that day. If they had a story of something they had tried that didn't go well, he would "high five" them. Failure for Sara became about not trying, not about the outcome. Their father expressed disappointment if they didn't fail frequently because it revealed they were hesitant to try anything new. This is a lesson for you. Instead of being afraid of failure, look forward to failing every day. Also, try to enjoy it because it's part of the success process. Without failure, there can be no success.

I hope you have learned a lot from my story. My team and I are here for you to help you Make More so you can Give More! Find me at www.AkbarSheikh.com

Akbar

# Epilogue

Now it's time for you to invest in yourself. Think of the offers, the collective wisdom represented in these chapters, and avail yourself of the expertise, heart, and experience of these driven, highly successful Dad-author-entrepreneurs. They have been where you are. They are here to serve so that you, in turn, may also serve - because the world really needs us right now! They are here to inspire you so that you, in turn, may inspire others to take action and turn your big dreams into reality.

As you've met the wonderful authors in this book - extremely accomplished influencers - I hope you have recognized some themes. First, as we remember our own, we are reminded that fathers matter, a lot! Second, most of us thought we were headed one way only to have life throw us one or more curve-balls, redirecting our paths significantly. Third, we have failed - fallen hard, disappointed ourselves or our family, felt lost, struggled for direction, caused financial stress - and ended up being so much stronger and focused as a result of those lessons. Fourth, each of us has chosen to forego a paycheck in exchange for living intentionally and deliberately. Finally, each of us is driven by our desire to make a difference, make an impact, and serve - and to do so has been a scary, uncomfortable, and deliberate choice to grow outside our comfort zones.

As entrepreneurial parents, we give our kids the gift of choice. They don't have to follow our path but the option is definitely open to them to live life on their terms. We firmly believe that the more we step into who we are, who we serve, and why, the more our horizons expand, and the more we find ourselves presented with new challenges. What's different now for each of us - and what each of us wants for you to feel - is that we believe 100% and more, that our big ginormous glorious dreams are possible. That we are possible!

We are Million Dollar Dads. We believe in our Million Dollar Stories and we believe you, too, are here to serve your readers and clients by using your unique experiences and expertise to offer them immediate relief, hope, and transformation because someone, somewhere, right now, is waiting desperately for YOU to provide a solution to their pain!

We are here to help you and to celebrate your journey. Thank you for sharing your time with us. If you found value in these stories, please take a minute and leave a review on Amazon - and tell a friend to buy this book. And of course, reach out to any of us about affiliate opportunities. *Your* Million Dollar Story begins with clarity and action. It is your time to act and it is your time to recognize *you are exactly where you are meant to be!*

My wish for you is that these stories nourish your belief, providing you with the courage to keep going in pursuit of your dreams - even if your dreams are forced in a new direction. I invite you to discover how collectively we, as these authors demonstrate, may use our unique stories and gifts, at any age, to change the world in small or large measure.

These authors have also shown we can't do it alone. They want to help you so be sure you take advantage of all the links and resources provided to you throughout these pages. Action matters - reach out today!

# About the Authors

# Preston Anderson

Preston is a seasoned tax planner and began his career in accounting, gaining unparalleled experience in the tax space, while also establishing himself as a respected CPA. He has worked in the tax and accounting industry for 17 years. He has developed The Upside Down Tax Method, a proven method to help entrepreneurs strategically cut their tax bills while putting more cash in their pockets. He is committed to continuing honing his skills to be able to serve his clients at ever-higher levels. Preston is passionate about guiding his clients to increase their net worth using the tax code, and removing the stress that the IRS can bring. His clients call him a tax genie. Preston is proud to call Chicago home. If you want help, reach out! Anderson.Tax

## Chris Baden

Chris is typically thinking about building three things at any given moment: a life-long marriage, a world-impacting family, and multi-million dollar businesses. In the last five years, Chris has been an equity partner in three different businesses in three different industries (Insurance, e-Comm, and Software) that grossed at least $1 Million per year in revenue. None of this would have been possible if it wasn't for one key skill he developed... Prospecting! Chris often refers to it as Purpose Driven Prospecting which emphasizes building new quality connections for maximum lifetime value. While business is growing, so is his family! Chris is a father of three as his brand new baby girl just arrived! Outside of business, Chris and his wife, Beth, competed on the hit TV Show "American Ninja Warrior!" If you are interested in working with Chris, connect with him here - SalesAscenders.com

# Eric Beer

Founder & CEO of Universal Marketing Partners. Serial Entrepreneur, Expert Affiliate Marketer, Lead Generation, Digital Marketer looking to share his knowledge with the world and add meaning to his efforts. Universal Marketing Partners (UMP) is a global marketing technology company that helps brands "start conversations" and "close conversions". The core of UMP's approach centers on harnessing the power of data collected from marketing activities to then inform the execution of media buying events. By building an ecosystem that integrates actionable data across the product lines, UMP effectively drives a conversation into a conversion and therefore consistently delivers clients outstanding ROI results. Eric is also the host of the Performance Marketing Podcast.

# James Golden

James Golden is the Founder and CEO of the Pavement Management Group and Chief Action Officer of JG3 Consulting. He got his start in pavement management working under a civil engineer and mentor at the age of 19. What began as a part-time job performing roadway condition assessments turned into a 22-year career, plus a passion for helping municipalities across the US save taxpayer dollars, maximize their annual budget, and increase the conditions of their roadway networks. When he is not advocating for roadway preservation,

James enjoys helping others in the constant pursuit of becoming the best version of themselves through personal and group coaching and his "Good to Goalden" podcast. The road to hitting your next level is just a click away. Get started today by joining James's free Facebook Group, The Golden Collective. James currently resides in Ohio with his wife Jamie, and their five kids: Dillon, Jaden, Michaela, Caden, and Emersen.

## Cody Loughlin

I am the Host of Money Talkers Podcast for parents who want successful children. I am also an individual who loves a challenge and a problem-solving opportunity. I have a diverse background in entrepreneurship, internet marketing, management, finance, and training. Having owned multiple successful companies and worked as a commercial banker, I can appreciate the perspective and challenges for both sides to obtain success. I believe that all individuals and processes in a company have a major impact on results. My mission statement is, "To receive exceptional results by consistently living by principles and values." If you want help talking money with your kids, reach out here www.TheMoneyTalkers.com

# Evans Putman

Evans is a coach and consultant who helps purpose-driven entrepreneurs and changemakers create profitable, scalable dream client businesses that align with their core values, serve their ideal customers, and turn their missions into movements. He has over 20 years of experience building successful businesses as an online entrepreneur, and his training has been featured in ClickFunnels Founder Russell Brunson's high-ticket coaching program. Evans' 7-Figure Podcast Blueprint gives coaches, consultants, course creators, and other expert entrepreneurs a proven system to turn a podcast into an automated traffic, leads, and high-ticket sales machine. He is also the host of the Infinite Impact Radio podcast and creator of the Infinite Impact Method™. Learn more and get your blueprint to increase income, ignite impact, and transform lives at www. EvansPutman.com

# Akbar Sheikh

Akbar Sheikh is a #1 International Best-Selling author, speaker, and master of the 7 Ethical Principles of Persuasion. He has helped eight funnels hit 7-figures. He is also a father and philanthropist with a concentration on orphans and giving the gift of vision to blind children. He is on a mission to create a massive impact through coaching and believes that as people earn more, they can give more - to their families, communities, and favorite charities - hence, making the world a better place. If you want his help to make more to give more, reach out to him here - www.AkbarSheikh.com.

# Jamie Wolf

Jamie Wolf, MBA, is CEO and President of **Million Dollar Story Agency** and Owner of Wolf Tide Publishing. She produced this book for its authors and in just twelve months, her Agency helped almost forty entrepreneurs become Best Selling published authors. If you want to make more sales and position yourself as an expert quickly - even if you are not a writer - we have a unique proprietary system that will instantly boost your credibility and sales; it's like you're getting a commercial during the Super Bowl!

If you've always wanted to get your book out to the world fast and to be a published Best Selling author and a major verified influencer with a large distribution network, connect with Jamie at MillionDollarStory.co! Even if you feel you can't write or don't have time, she can help you!

One way to get that Blue Checkmark on IG and FB without carving out too much time - **so you can boost your status, easily attract new customers, and warrant premium pricing** - is to become a Best Selling author. I'm guessing you have a story worth sharing! I've got an easy way for you to do just that while being featured strategically alongside other influencers to multiply your audience and list with no extra effort even in these crazy times.

If the thought of writing a book keeps surfacing but you aren't sure how to start (or finish) I invite you to join my free Facebook™ group called the *"Influencer Circle."* It's a group I share with fellow mission-and-success driven entrepreneurs who are committed to growing their influence, status, and client base in order to make a bigger impact and change more lives. Be sure to request to join Influencer Circle You can also listen to powerful stories filled with action items at Million Dollar PIVOT, on iTunes and other podcast sites.